How to Start
Lay-Shepherding Ministries

How to Start
Lay-Shepherding Ministries

Charles A. Ver Straten

Baker Book House
Grand Rapids, Michigan 49506

Copyright 1983 by
Baker Book House Company

ISBN: 0-8010-9290-6

First printing, April 1983
Second printing, December 1983

Printed in the United States of America

To the deacons and deaconesses
who have shared with the ministry
of pastoral care with me.

You have been my partners
in shepherding God's people.

This is your story.
I thank you and salute you.

67739

Contents

Introduction

An unrealistic expectation of the ministry and the role of the senior pastor exists in church life today. Sometimes it is found in the pastor himself. While he may have been a superstar in years past, he is now measuring himself by remote memory. Tormenting expectations may gain impetus by the recall of remarks, attitudes or instructions absorbed in seminary. These contain a heavy "oughtness" of responsibility with eternal consequences. No one has suggested that he might possibly be taking himself too seriously.

The church he serves, whatever the size, will have more unrealistic expectations of his ministry. The congregation's standard is for a man ten-feet tall. Care for the church building as well as the people, visitation, community evangelism, committees, youth activities, Sunday school, and even social affairs, somehow fall under his unwritten job description.

This man is a perfect set-up for what happens next. Both the pastor and his church have imagined a role that is unreachable and untenable. He feels that he must not be a disappointment. He will become the ubiquitous pastor. One dictionary defines *ubiquitous:* ". . . existing or being everywhere, omnipresent."

Temporarily, verbal applause from the congregation will supply nourishment for his hungry ego with its human need of affirmation. They say: "I don't see how you do it all. You're always around. Mr. Everywhere. No matter how busy, you always make time."

In the end, a ubiquitous style of leadership is usually erosive and destructive to the effectiveness of such a pastor. Degenerative effects first puff him up, then burn him out.

Cecil Murphy, writing in the Minister's Workshop column of *Christianity Today,* cited a minister with a leadership style like this:

> Gene became pastor of a congregation with a membership listed as nearly 600 but regular attendance of 125. Within six months, Gene had activities humming. Attendance picked up, new programs abounded. The budget doubled in three years. But in the fifth year, Gene moved to a different church. The church is back to an average attendance of 125, much like it was before Gene came on the scene. "In a lot of ways he hurt the church," a member said. "He kept everything in his grip. Nothing went on without his approval."[1]

His leadership style was based on an erroneous assumption, that the ministry was his. A scriptural injunction tells that ministry was intended to be the people's, and that the pastor is to train them. ". . . and some to be pastors and teachers, to prepare God's people for works of service, so that the body of Christ may be built up" (Eph. 4:11-12).

When unscriptural and unrealistic expectations for ministry are lived out by the pastor and congregation, the ultimate effect will be erosive. The long-term health of the church will suffer.

This is particularly true when the shepherding life of a church is scrutinized. In the majority of situations, pastoral care and spiritual nurture of the congregation is exclusively the responsibility of the senior pastor. If his leadership style is ubiquitous, a vital part of his ministry will suffer neglect.

He will constantly be rediscovering that he cannot be everywhere at all times. A good pastor looks for ways to help his people grow, while numerous, urgent, but less important matters demand prime time. Their urgency may crowd out his central ministry of nurturing spiritual growth.

1. *Christianity Today,* December 15, 1978, p. 32.

When the senior pastor usurps for himself the role of shepherding, there are short- and long-range degenerative effects.

The laity is not prepared or equipped for works of service in building up the body as intended. The members are deprived of becoming the Lord's instruments of meaningful service. Their potential usefulness for God is stymied.

Those who would be served and nurtured suffer. With inadequate shepherding care, those in the body needing discipleship, encouragement, and exhortation fail to grow.

The ubiquitous pastor usually faces burn out after a ministry of five or six years. When a change of churches and pastorates appears to be his only solution for finding release from unbearable strain, he bails out and departs.

Termination is a terrible disservice because he leaves a shepherdless flock. He taught them to depend on him alone. Because he retained the exclusive right to shepherd, they are left unprepared to fend for themselves.

A transfer of confidence to another shepherd takes one-and-a-half to two years. Only then will the next pastor lead people into a nurturing relationship producing a similar rate of growth.

Warning words of Jesus should cause the pastor reconsideration.

> The hired hand is not the shepherd who owns the sheep. So when he sees the wolf coming, he abandons the sheep and runs away. Then the wolf attacks the flock and scatters it. The man runs away because he is a hired hand and cares nothing for the sheep (John 10:12-13).

If a minister chooses to have a series of short pastorates, he must provide pastoral care in the congregations after he is gone.

A minister, who sees his primary gifts in areas other than shepherding, needs a source of people to minister as shepherds.

Care by a trained lay person may be more effective than by the senior pastor himself. The member needing nurture identifies more readily with a lay person than a professional clergyman, who may be regarded as too busy to spend extra time. If the pastor should leave for another church, the lay shepherds will be there to provide continuity. The laity will be blessed when in direct service as God's instruments.

In his book, *Everyone A Minister,* Oscar Feucht has observed rightfully:

> An adequate ministry is not a one man ministry. It is not even a corps of associated pastors. It is the whole church, congregation by congregation, mobilized and trained for mission. Only this strategy is adequate.[2]

2. Oscar E. Feucht, *Everyone A Minister* (Philadelphia: Westminster Press, 1974), p. 80.

1

Scattering Sheep and a Stressful Shepherd

My congregation had grown from 175 people to more than 600 in seven years. On paper it appeared to be a successful church. As the senior pastor, I was frustrated, overextended, and ready to resign.

My greatest strength had proved to be my undoing. God had given me a pastor's heart to care deeply for people. This intimate shepherding care had been a major factor in attracting people to the church. It continued as a catalyst for growth.

During these years, the church had become too much for me. The size of the flock had grown unwieldy for my style of ministering. I was caught in the scriptural parallel when Jethro advised Moses.

> What you are doing is not good. You and these people who come to you will only wear yourselves out. The work is too heavy for you; you cannot handle it alone (Exod. 18:17-18).

Thousands of years later in Denver, Colorado, I couldn't handle it alone.

This modern-day Moses began to look to the senior pastors of Denver's largest churches. I wanted to learn how they had coped with the problem of adequate pastoral care for their growing congregations. In addition, I sent a questionnaire on the subject to each of the larger churches of my denomination.

Answers that I received were discouraging. Without exception, the replies indicated that as a congregation grew beyond 300-500 in numerical size, there was a decreasing pastoral care ministry.

Some families of our membership were scattering to other churches. The reason they gave was always the same, "The Mission Hills Church is getting too big. It's no longer the warm, intimate, caring church it was, back when we became a part of it."

They were right. I wavered on the verge of wanting to leave, too. I had a conviction that ideal shepherding was possible only in a smaller church. There was agreement with Carl S. Dudley, who wrote in *Christian Ministry:*

> A small church cannot grow in membership without giving up something very precious, the basic satisfaction that everyone knows or knows about someone else. This intimacy is not an accident, since the essential character of the small church is this capacity to know and care about others.[1]

I was ready to leave this larger, apparently successful church for a smaller one. If I couldn't handle it alone, I should resign.

My circumstances and my error have been described poignantly by Jay Adams.

> When the pastor on his own tries to do the work of an entire congregation . . . he fails because he spreads himself too thin, trying to do too much as one person. It is nothing less than pride for any one individual to think that he is capable of doing what God said is the work of an entire congregation. He fails also as a pastor-teacher. In spreading himself so thinly over the works of evangelism, as well as that of shepherding, and of teaching, he does none of those well. His sermons suffer, his members are not cared for, and even the fruit of the evangelism is minimal.[2]

1. Carl S. Dudley, "Membership Growth, The Impossible Necessity." *Christian Ministry,* Vol. 8, No. 4, July, 1977.
2. Jay E. Adams, *Pastoral Leadership* (Grand Rapids: Baker Book House, 1975), p. 25.

I was being prepared to apply a lesson learned while ranching in Wyoming. God's plan was to change me from a shepherd to a ranch foreman.

My knowledge of the ways of sheep has provided background for sermon illustrations through the years. I had observed that God's people have many similarities to sheep. Now, I was to apply shepherding practices to my leadership as the senior pastor in a larger church.

The typical large sheep ranch in Wyoming divides its sheep into bands of one thousand ewes. Each band of ewes, with their lambs, is assigned to a solitary shepherd. These men, from Mexico, speak little English. They are given a trained sheep dog, a small sheep wagon in which they live alone, cook, and sleep.

Bands of sheep are dispersed on various sections of a ranch, with the location of each sheep wagon marking the bedding area for that flock. The sheep graze in the nearby grass. The wagon is located within traveling distance of a windmill. Sheep are herded there for water each day. At night they are bedded near the wagon, where the herder listens for coyotes and bands of wild dogs. After several days of feeding and browsing, the grass is grazed short, and it is time to move to greener pastures.

A large ranch has many bands of sheep. The ranch foreman manages the entire operation. It is his responsibility to oversee the shepherds with their dispersed bands. He checks the grass, locates a new grazing area, determines the distance from water, while arranging for the wagon's setting in a safe bedding ground. He instructs the shepherd in the care of the sheep, examining their health, progress, and general well-being.

The ranch foreman's style of leadership anticipates increase in the flocks. Numerical growth, production of wool, fat lambs that weigh well in the fall, are the money-making bottom line.

The shepherd views numerical growth from a different perspective than the foreman. A high rate of multiple births causes him frustration. He knows there is a limit to the number of sheep he can personally tend even if his workload is increased.

From my sheep ranch upbringing in Wyoming, there was a lesson for me. As the senior pastor of a suburban church, I had become a shepherd deeply worried about neglected and scattering sheep. I was ready to resign, while the Lord was readying me for reassignment. He was preparing me for a promotion on the same ranch. Soon I would begin to view myself in a different role.

2

Scanning for Assistance

In reflection, like the rapid recall of a drowning man, I came to realize that overextension had been accumulating for several years.

The effective performance for my intimate style of ministering peaked when the congregation reached 250 members. Shortly after, the time of stress began. My first response was to try harder. More hours were spent while efforts were increased. Leisure and family time were decreased. But this was only a temporary, stopgap measure. Numbers of people needing a shepherding ministry continued to increase.

Next I went to seminars on time management. My response to overextension was to shape up, get more mileage out of my life! It was a helpful and needed discipline, but it did not meet the needs of our growing church. I kept reading and seeking advice.

The building of a multiple staff, in the form of seminary trained professional clergymen, seemed the next logical step. I was assured that the added financial cost was really an investment that would soon take care of itself.

Any discussion of adding staff members brings up the question of finances. With an all-too-tight budget, how can a church even consider adding another staff member? . . . Churches with a healthy growth pattern take an enlightened step of faith. Their experience shows that a capable staff member will result in more families that tithe. In two years, the additional income will underwrite his salary and an expanded program. So, church leaders trust the Lord and challenge their people to provide the finances for the initial salary.[1]

At the time I was facing my own personal crisis, I led the church in seeking pastoral assistants. I gave considerable leadership to those selections. Search committees explored the needs, looking for balance and complement. We were forming a team. Finally we selected two men gifted in particular ministries needed in the church. First, we moved a seminary student, who had served as part-time youth pastor, into a full-time Minister of Music/Youth Pastor position. Then we hired a second man to serve as Christian Education/Church Administrator.

I had been convinced by counsel and reading that the addition of more members to the pastoral staff would result in a shared shepherding ministry.

This was a wrong assumption. I soon discovered that specialized associates do not necessarily contribute to the pastoral care ministry. Our new men activated the areas where their gifts and talents were. Their assistance in pastoral care was minimal.

My young associates were gifted and motivated men. They created new quality programs for their specialized ministries. These attracted more people. My dilemma was compounded by many more people who were being added to our congregation. Each one needed pastoral care. This modern-day Moses was overwhelmed.

I had not yet read the wise observation of Jay Adams.

. . . It may seem obvious that while there are advantages (fellowship, the power of specialization, etc.) there are also disadvantages to a multiple staff ministry. Perhaps the greatest is this: thinking that the addition of specialized staff members itself will serve the needs of a growing large congregation. When "minister of music" . . . "of youth," and "of visitation," etc. are added, that does not necessarily mean that the congregation will be

---

1. *Christianity Today*, March 24, 1978, p. 38.

served better. . . . When a congregation reaches the size of 800-1000 members, it still does not receive adequate *pastoral* work by the addition of a "minister of music" or a "minister of youth." What is needed is the addition of three or four more "ministers of sheep!" It is a rare congregation that sees this and sufficiently provides for the need.[2]

While the general work of the church was enhanced by the addition of the gifted staff associates, the ministry of shepherding remained the responsibility of the senior pastor. My primary gift in this area caused other staff members to depend on me for this ministry.

I was convinced that the Holy Spirit gifts the leadership with the full complement of charisms needed to minister to the whole body. The logical step was to add individuals who were specialists in pastoral care because of gifts and training. This seemed the obvious move to take. It was consistent with my long-range goal for providing complete ministerial leadership as the church grew. I began to interview for a visitation pastor.

Two factors made me hesitate. In retrospect, I recognize them as God's providential leading. First was the financial consideration. Though the church was overextended financially, the need was great. Even one visitation pastor would only be band-aid treatment. I needed three or four full-time shepherds immediately.

The second reservation was received during the process of scrutinizing some of the larger churches in the Denver area. I observed a correlation between the addition of each pastoral staff person with a corresponding decrease in the participation of lay people. The increase of staff people was matched by a decrease in lay involvement. I wondered if this contributed to the escalation of spectatorism in these larger churches.

We needed a church functioning as a participatory body, with each member active. This is the New Testament standard for a congregation. I was convinced that this was the type of church to minister spiritual health to people in a suburban community.

2. Adams, *Pastoral Leadership*, p. 55.

Now it is most apparent from Ephesians 4 that all Christians are "in the ministry." . . . When the ministry was thus left to the professionals there was nothing left for the people to do other than come to church and listen. They were told that it was their responsibility to bring the world into the church building to hear the pastor preach the gospel. Soon Christianity became nothing but a spectator sport, very much akin to the definition of football—22 men down on the field, desperately in need of rest, and 20 thousand in the grandstands, desperately in need of exercise![3]

I was left with one option. There remained a source for shepherding assistance, the laity of the Mission Hills Church.

I will be using the modern definitions of "laity" and "clergy." Today the term *clergy* is applied to one vocationally trained and employed in Christian ministry. When that vocational commitment ceases, even if he is ordained, he is no longer "clergy." The term *laity* is applied to the believer not financially reimbursed for his ministry.

Though this is the most prevalent understanding of these terms, such a distinction is not found in the New Testament.

The word "lay" goes back to the Greek word *laikos.* . . . It means originally: belonging to the *"laos";* that is the chosen people of God, both in the Old and New Testament.[4]

This term *"laos"* refers to all the people of God. Peter says: "But you are a chosen people, a royal priesthood, a holy nation, a people belonging to God. . . . Once you were not a people, but now you are the people of God" (I Peter 2:9-10).

In the New Testament sense all of God's people are His called people. They are God's "clergy" in the world.

The word "clergy" is derived from the Greek word *kleros.* . . . It is related to the verb "call" and is employed in the Greek New

3. Ray C. Stedman, *Body Life* (Glendale: Regal Books, 1972), pp. 78, 79.
4. Hendrick Kraemer, *A Theology of the Laity* (Philadelphia: Westminster Press, 1958), p. 49.

Testament when referring to the Holy Spirit calling a person by the Gospel into the Christian Fellowship of the church.[5]

Therefore, modern usage of the terms *laity* and *clergy* with their currently accepted meanings, have use only as functional terms. They have limited relationship to New Testament teachings. Usage must always be subordinate to biblical teachings of priesthood of all believers.

My remaining option for immediate shepherding assistance was the recruitment of lay people, who had demonstrated gifts of shepherding care. A step in that direction seemed a move away from dependency on the professional staff. We needed to stop the shift toward spectatorism occurring in the church. The New Testament teaching of the priesthood of all believers was our final benediction. Development of lay shepherds for a pastoral care ministry dovetailed perfectly with the priesthood of all believers.

Propositions for my plan of operation unfolded as a result of five conclusions.

All people, those in suburbia particularly, need the shepherding ministry of God. They will respond to God through care extended to them by Christ's church in Christ's name.

Spiritual growth is most productive in a caring community which provides pastoral leadership. Nurture, feeding, and care are offered through adequate personal shepherding.

Adequate shepherding care cannot be a one-man ministry. It must be an apportioned, shared service. Part of the responsibility must be delegated to others. "Men who fear God, trustworthy men who hate dishonest gain" (Exod. 18:21).

Most churches are financially unable to provide a large enough staff of associates to meet shepherding needs of the congregation.

There is a multiplicity of qualified lay persons with gifts related to the ministry of shepherding who can be a better source of competent pastoral service than a few staff members.

5. Feucht, *Everyone a Minister,* p. 57.

The volunteer status of the lay shepherd eliminates the idea that he is working for the congregation.

I had discovered the source of assistance at a very critical juncture in my pastoral career.

The process of my reassignment was now in its initial stages. God was unfolding His plan to broaden my horizons. He was going to make me a ranch foreman.

3

A Scheme for Lay Shepherding

I was beginning to look like a senior pastor. My hair had turned white, and character lines were becoming more deeply etched on my face. Overextension in my ministry seemed to contribute to all of this.

Finally, I concluded that the sole style of ministry simply wouldn't work in a larger church. Sharing the shepherding ministry with lay people seemed the correct course.

Numerous questions and necessary decisions crowded in. Who should be chosen? How many shepherds would be enough in the beginning phase? How should they be trained and mobilized?

The added responsibility of training others seemed overwhelming. Again I was tempted to think that it would still be so much easier to resign than remain.

The foundation for lay shepherding at the Mission Hills Church was laid in study and evaluation of similar programs in nationally prominent churches.

Dr. David Bailey, Minister of Pastoral Care at Garden Grove (California) Community Church, invited me to be his house guest. During those days I studied the well-organized Lay Ministers Pastoral Care Program of that superchurch.

During one interview, David Bailey described the role of lay minister in his church.

Our entire pastoral care is designed to relate the people of the church to their Lay Minister. He is responsible to be in contact

21

with them personally through visiting in their homes, telephoning, and personal letters. The Lay Minister is to be on the alert to greet the people assigned to him as he sees them in church. He is to notice the ones he does not see and contact them. The Lay Ministers are assistants to the Ministers in sharing the concern of Christ's church for each member.[1]

Garden Grove, like most churches studied, chooses its lay ministers by recruitment of volunteers. Candidates are placed in a training program; they can serve as lay minister interns while they study. Upon completion of the program, they receive the Certificate of Credentialed Lay Minister.

The Garden Grove Program is organized on a geographic basis. Orange County plus parts of Los Angeles County are divided into zones. Member-families are pinpointed in areas and assigned to a Zone Lay Minister who lives near by. He is responsible to each family. Quarterly contacts are suggested. Accountability is built into the system. The Zone Lay Minister reports to a Division Lay Minister, he to an Area Lay Minister, who advises the salaried Minister of Pastoral Care.

Calvary Temple of Denver, Colorado, has a similar program, called the Lay Shepherd Ministry. People are recruited or volunteer to serve. Attendance at a twelve-hour Laymen's Educational Advancement and Development Course is required. After that course is completed, the trainee is recognized as a Lay Shepherd.

The organizational structure of Calvary Temple's Lay Shepherd Ministry is patterned after the Garden Grove Program. The city of Denver is divided into geographic sectors. Accountability is achieved through a similar pyramid of supervision.

A different approach to lay shepherding is used by the Wooddale Baptist Church in the Minneapolis area. Within the larger church, small congregations are set up like the adult Sunday school classes. Each small congregation has a teacher who functions as a pastor. These congregations are used as channels of communication for many activities of the church. They are cen-

---

1. Interview with David D. Bailey, Minister of Pastoral Care, Garden Grove Community Church, Garden Grove, California, January 26, 1979.

ters of fellowship and spiritual growth, where people know and pray for each other.

In Whittier, California, Dan Baumann, the senior minister of the Whittier Area Baptist Fellowship, describes a successful care ministry of that church:

> *Circles of Concern.* The Congregation is broken down into twenty-five circles which meet on a regular basis. Membership is voluntary; no one is forced to participate. Each circle averages about seven families who meet monthly for a study night. One month they gather in the twenty-five homes for Bible Study, discussion, sharing and prayer. The next month at church for a meeting of adults only. These sessions occur on Wednesday. A social night is conducted by each circle every month. The nature of the socials is determined by the individual circles. Groupings change each year to encourage people to make new friends and to cut down the likelihood of cliques. Circle leaders are chosen because of their commitment to a caring ministry. It is the responsibility of these individuals to pray for each member of their circle at least once a week, to lead the studies and socials, to keep in regular contact with all members . . . visit sick and delinquent members, and communicate emergent needs to the pastoral staff.[2]

I studied smaller churches as well. Don Fuller is the sole pastor of Grace Baptist Church in Anaconda, Montana. His wife is his personal secretary on a volunteer basis. Grace Baptist averages 100 people in worship services.

In the fall of 1976, this pastor organized nine teams each having a deacon and his wife. These teams lead nine prayer/share groups, which include nonmember families as well as member families. The husband, wife and children are assigned to the same group. Each deacon with his wife has approximately ten households assigned to them.

The groups view their deacon and his wife as associates in ministry with the pastor. Weekly prayer/share meetings include

---

2. Dan Baumann, *All Originality Makes a Dull Church* (Santa Ana: Vision House Publishers, 1976), pp. 107, 108.

children as well as adults. Groups select their own time and place of meeting. Different groups meet different nights of the week, and attendance varies from four to twenty. Everyone uses the prayer/share guide, written by Pastor Fuller, edited and mimeographed by Mrs. Fuller, and placed in the bulletin on Sunday.

I learned that shared shepherding isn't just for larger churches where the senior pastor can no longer handle the pastoral ministry alone. It is a biblical principle of leadership which can multiply the effectiveness of a solo pastor in a smaller church. Don Fuller has become a ranch foreman in a church of 150 members. In reflection, I wish that I had learned these lessons earlier to use in the small churches of my earlier pastorates.

From research and study of these churches plus others, from extensive reading on care ministries and small groups, a plan for a lay-shepherding ministry was developing. God was showing me a schematic for Mission Hills Church.

Though I realized there were many varying philosophies, creative approaches, and differing ideas with respect to lay shepherding, it was now time to pick and choose. Questions arose that demanded decisions.

1. Who were to be the lay shepherds? It seemed wise to me to train people who had been elected by the congregation to offices that were associated with spiritual leadership. Deacons, rather than ones who might volunteer, seemed best positioned to train for a lay-shepherding ministry.

The pastor is to be the initial enlister and trainer of his people until a new breed is ready to carry on that work. The best place for him to begin is with the existing leadership of the church — the elders and/or the deacons. These in turn will shortly thereafter reproduce themselves in the lives of others in the congregation. This might be costly at the onset, in terms of time and energy, but it will doubtless produce abundant and enduring fruit.[3]

3. Synesio Lyra, Jr., *A New Laity* (Garden Grove, Ca.: Lay Ministry Training Center), p. 13.

Some years prior, a Coordinating Board composed of moderator, senior pastor, four board chairmen (including the deacon chairman), had been constituted as the executive board of the church. Therefore, the Board of Deacons was free to major in spiritual ministries. A minor change shifted the selection of deaconesses, so that those nominated had to be the wives of deacons. This ensured the necessary husband-wife combinations.

I settled on the term *Little Flock* as the formal name for each of the shepherding groups. In my thinking, there was a parallel between separating the people of the congregation into Little Flocks like the various bands of sheep under one herder on the Wyoming plains.

2. What type of training was to be given? To teach lay people what I had learned about shepherding from twenty-three years in the pastorate would take more than a few initial lessons.

I could see pouring my life into lay shepherds so they could share the ministry with me. The training would need to include formal teaching, on-the-job experience and an associational discipling with me. This would require a continual program, possibly weekly, for a good part of the year.

3. Who should be included in the shepherding ministry? The congregation who had used the adult Sunday school class plan had many advantages. A primary disadvantage is that it did not extend to the entire membership. Non-Sunday school attenders were excluded. Teachers and workers in other departments of the Sunday school could be reached in a limited manner.

The "circles of concern" plan has the same basic disadvantage. Including only those who volunteer to be a part of the ministry will miss a percentage of the membership. These, intentionally, or by default, exclude themselves. Often reserved, timid, non-gregarious people have more need for shepherding care and a support group than the natural joiners. They are reluctant to sign up to be a part of a new and unknown ministry.

I decided that Little Flocks should include every household in the church regardless of individual church membership or commitment to Christ. If everyone was to be included under the umbrella of shepherding care, assignment seemed the only workable procedure.

Each member family would be assigned to a Little Flock under the pastoral care of a designated husband/wife shepherding team. I knew that a small percentage of those assigned would probably be inactive in Little Flock functions. In spite of a reluctance to participate, these individuals would benefit by having a lay pastor and his wife to minister to them.

4. How to determine the assignment of people to their respective Little Flocks was a difficult decision. Because the Mission Hills Church ministers to a suburban area, most of the membership lives within a three-mile radius of the church. Forming the groups on the basis of geography was pointless. I knew that guidelines had to be relational, with careful formation.

Relationships needed to be vertical in respect to the lay shepherd leadership and horizontal in reference to flock members. Interrelating as cohesion, would determine whether the Little Flock would form a meaningful unit.

Should the shepherding group be homogeneous in composition? Should the singles, elderly, young parents, professionals, and blue-collar employees be placed in groups with others of similar circumstances and common interests? Or, should each Little Flock be a heterogeneous group, composed of people who represented a cross-section of the congregation?

It seemed advisable to choose the latter option. We arranged the placing in the Little Flocks people of all ages, differing income levels, dissimilar vocational pursuits, and varying marital status. This has required more effort for the husband/wife teams to effect relationships with unlike Little Flock members.

Time has proved this the correct course for many reasons. Single-parent mothers and their children had men and fathers in their Little Flock to relate to. Single and divorced people were included in family affairs. The elderly were brought into the mainstream of the church. This all outweighed the early difficulties in making each group a cohesive whole.

During the first year of the shepherding ministry, a measure of choice was given to church members. Each household received a mailed form with the names of the lay shepherds listed. Members were asked to circle the names of three deacons they could relate to. (Few realized the significance of the plans that were being made, and only twenty-seven percent of the forms were returned.)

Lay-shepherding teams were asked to present the names of six-member households they would like to have in their Little Flocks. There was some duplication that had to be matched with requests from the returned forms.

I chose not to use a draft. A draft by deacons for shepherding group members would have created a climate of choosing up sides. Because the guidelines were relational, the selection required careful study and prayer.

After requests by the membership and the lay-shepherding teams were honored, the chairman of the Board of Deacons, the chairwoman of the Board of Deaconesses, and I finished the task. We spent several hours studying the remaining names and the composition of each Little Flock. We looked for balance.

Considerable prayer went into that final placement. After all, "Man looks at the outward appearance, but the LORD looks at the heart" (I Samuel 16:7). Christ our Shepherd knew which lay shepherd could best minister to each of His sheep.

Approximately twelve households were placed in each Little Flock. Flocks including households representing single people were increased.

The basic plan was ready. The congregation and the lay shepherds had been initially prepared. The scheme for sharing the shepherding ministry was developing.

Study, planning, preparation, and prayer had started the transformation. I was excited. Everywhere I looked, I saw the potential of lay people with the opportunity of spiritual service for their God. My growing congregation had the prospect of receiving the shepherding it needed.

I was beginning to be a ranch foreman.

4

Training Shapes Lay Shepherds

Deacon watch-care lists are not new in church circles. Usually they are mimeographed, assigned, and dutifully placed in the deacon notebook. The deacon is aware that he has a spiritual responsibility for the people assigned to him. Frequently, the list remains in the notebook and only occasionally pricks the conscience of the deacon.

I realized that the whole project might not go farther than the composition of lists with their assignment to deacon-deaconess teams. How could I motivate the deacons and deaconesses into an active and meaningful lay-shepherding ministry?

Two things were necessary. First, I would model my own shepherding as an example. I needed to be the master teacher. Second, I would need to develop a trial-and-error process so that they could teach themselves. This required frequent exposure of my life to theirs. This would take a great amount of time and proximity.

I chose a weekly training period as the most practical means of pouring my experiences into the lives of trainees. The deacons and deaconesses met with me at church, in the fireside room, around tables, each Wednesday evening during the regular mid-week service time. The lay-shepherd training class was designed in nine-month increments, from September through May.

At the time of writing, the training program is concluding its third year. As the program progressed, different approaches and

29

emphases were required. Each training year revealed weaknesses requiring revision.

This chapter will give an overview of the lay-shepherd training of those three years. Twelve husband-wife teams were enrolled in the first training year; sixteen in the second year of training; and nineteen teams have been enrolled in the current year.

The First Year

The weekly ninety-minute class session was aimed at training the deacons and deaconesses. They were to become proficient in shepherding skills while they were developing their own ministries to their Little Flocks.

Minimum requirements for Little Flock ministry provided a standard for each shepherding team:

1. There must be a corporate Little Flock gathering at least once each three months.
2. There must be the establishment of a meaningful pastoral relationship between the Lay Shepherd and each member of his Little Flock.
3. A hospital call must be made by the Lay Shepherd on each Little Flock member who is hospitalized.
4. An undershepherding team, husband and wife from the Little Flock, must be selected and trained as assistants in the ministry of the flock.
5. A home communion service, with the gathered Little Flock, is to be held in one of the homes at least once each year.[1]

On-the-job training with its weekly sessions produced several indirect benefits. The first five minutes of the class period were

1. Charles A. Ver Straten, "Changing Baptist Deacons Into Lay Shepherds" (Doctoral Dissertation, Denver: Conservative Baptist Theological Seminary, 1980), p. 104.

spent in report time. Lay shepherds shared corporate activities of their Little Flocks; they told about ministries of note with individual members. There was built-in accountability in completing assignments. The necessity of having something to share stimulated the ministries.

The second five minutes of each training class period were used for checking memorized verses with members (not their mates). Knowing one would be expected to recite to a fellow trainee was a good discipline and an effective spur. Frequent sharing by class members about new discoveries and developments in their devotional lives worked as a catalyst to others.

As the instructor, I wrote a notebook which became the training manual. It was a simple 5½-by-8½ inch, three-ring notebook bearing the name of the deacon or deaconess. All the printed materials were punched to fit the notebook. The deacons and deaconesses placed weekly handouts in designated sections. In three years of training, these notebooks have become valuable for reference and resource.

The notebooks contain seven sections: 1) Assignments, 2) Memorization, 3) Personal Growth, 4) Doctrine, 5) Little Flock Ministry, 6) How to Shepherd, and 7) Management Principles.

A summary of each section gives insight into the content of the first year's training program:

1. Assignments. This section received an update at the beginning of each three-month period of training. It listed the dates of the weekly meetings with exceptions, the memorization schedule, other assignments, and the general theme of each meeting.

2. Memorization. The Navigator's *Topical Memory System* was used. Verse cards were printed to be cut out and placed in each notebook. The *New International Version* was the translation used in the memory program and the training class. Each trainee began memorizing with no advantages because of a previous memorization. Also, a new translation forced a fresh look at verses learned by rote in childhood. Some mature-

appearing Christians began to admit years since they had committed any portion of the Bible to memory. They had been depending on a collection of verses memorized many years ago. Knowing they were expected to share their newly-memorized verse each week with a fellow trainee spurred them to plant God's word in their hearts and minds.

3. Doctrine. The necessity for instructing the lay shepherds and their wives in sound doctrine became evident in the initial stages of training. Modeling a life of godly character, as described in I Timothy 3, was not enough. It was not enough for the lay-shepherding team to provide a ministry of compassion. Paul instructed Timothy, "Watch your life and doctrine closely" (I Tim. 4:16). If the people were to be true shepherds, it was important to understand truthful doctrine, to recognize error, and be able to instruct the people under their care.

> Be shepherds of the church of God, which he bought with his own blood. I know that after I leave, savage wolves will come in among you and will not spare the flock. Even from your own number men will arise and distort the truth in order to draw away disciples after them. So be on your guard! (Acts 20:28-31)

The doctrinal section for the first half of the training year was based on the twelve articles of faith in the church's statement.

1. The Word of God
2. The Trinity
3. God the Father
4. Jesus Christ
5. The Holy Spirit
6. Regeneration
7. The Church
8. Christian Conduct
9. The Ordinances
10. Religious Liberty
11. Church Cooperation
12. The Last Things[2]

2. Appendix, p. 91. See "An Affirmation of Our Faith."

One-half hour of each training period (twelve weeks) was designated for the study of each of the articles in successive order.

Each of the twelve deacons was assigned one doctrinal area at the beginning of a quarter. On a given date, the trainee taught his doctrinal subject under the supervision of the senior pastor. A handout was prepared by the trainee and printed by the church office for distribution.

I was amazed at the benefits and pleased with the results. The teacher-deacon learned more than his students because of the time spent in mastering the subject and preparing for the lesson. Twelve deacons became knowledgeable in twelve important biblical doctrinal areas. Another advantage was the attention given to the lesson because of identification with the student teacher. Though the deacons would have expected sound teaching from their senior pastor, they listened better to a fellow layman. I admitted that the student teachers spent more hours in preparation than I might have, therefore probably instructing more thoroughly.

This course of study caused the deacons and their wives to be more interested in doctrine. They were more aware of the various nuances in theological meaning on the contemporary religious scene.

4. Personal Growth. This section included material for the devotional prayer life of the lay shepherd and received a primary emphasis the first year. Prayer sheets with a place to record the request, date asked, and date answered, were in the notebook.

As the instructor, I strongly encouraged each shepherd to pray for the people of his Little Flock. I shared the importance of prayers of intercession and how to develop a ministry of prayer. Samuel's example and words were basic, "As for me, far be it from me that I should sin against the LORD by failing to pray for you" (I Sam. 12:23).

InterVarsity's guidebook for daily devotions, *Quiet Time*,[3] was

3. *Quiet Time* (Downers Grove: InterVarsity Press, 1977).

given to each shepherding team at the initiation of the program to foster systematic devotions in the lives of the lay shepherds.

For several months the following guide for using the Bible at daily devotional time was employed. Paragraph assignments in scripture were made for each day so that the students and I would be using the same passage. A standard form entitled "Paragraph Title Record" was prepared.[4]

Each week's completed forms were handed in for checking. I penned affirming and encouraging notes on them when merited. These forms were returned, when those of the following week were collected.

Initially, there was minor resistance by some class members. A few of the trainees felt that I was looking over their shoulders during their devotional time. Others thought it was too mechanical and robbed them of spontaneity. Eventually, all the students were cooperative enough to comply. Those who initially resisted admitted later that it was a needed discipline.

Other devotional materials and techniques were used. When the daily quiet time was well-established, the trainees were encouraged to develop their devotions in a manner that would assure spiritual growth.

5. Little Flocks. A listing of each of the Little Flocks appeared under its respective shepherding team. Each deacon and deaconess had a record of all the other Little Flocks and made additions as new members were assigned.

There were instructions about the selection, role, and duties, of the undershepherding lay teams. Each team was requested to select and recruit another husband-wife combination from their Little Flock. They would assist in the shepherding responsibilities of the group.

Undershepherds were invited to one weekly orientation meeting. They were told about the total shepherding program in general and the role of the undershepherds in particular. This group provided a reservoir of potential deacons and deaconesses who had been introduced to the Little Flock ministry.

---

4. Appendix 2, p. 94. See a sample "Paragraph Title Record" form.

Also included in this section were instructions in "Basic Requirements for Overseeing Little Flocks."[5]

6. How to Shepherd. This was the practical section of the notebook. I wrote much of the material from my own ranch experience and from many years as a shepherding pastor. This was applied to lay shepherding, converted into the form of weekly handouts, and placed in the notebook. The notebook section, "How to Shepherd," included the following studies.

1. The Shepherd is a *watchman*
2. The Shepherd is a *guard*
3. The Shepherd is a *guide*
4. The Shepherd is a *physician*
5. The Shepherd is a *rescuer*
6. The Shepherd is a *feeder of the sheep*
7. The Shepherd is a *lover of the sheep*[6]

As the first year of training progressed, handouts on evangelism, counseling in response to the invitation, hospital visitation, and case histories for study were added to this section of the notebook.

7. Management. Because the ministry of shepherding involves a considerable amount of time, it seemed wise to introduce some basic management principles. The teams needed to learn to prioritize their lives to handle the additional stresses that were occuring. This section was minor in comparison to others, but I was surprised at the enthusiastic interest.

Summary: The hours I spent in preparing notebook assignments and contents in advance of the class were many, as was the costly effort required in actual classroom training, but it was time well spent.

The wise pastor also recognizes that a vital part of his role as shepherd is the training of these lay shepherds. . . . This takes

5. Appendix 3, p. 95.
6. C. Ver Straten, "Shepherding Notebook" (Littleton, Co.: Mission Hills Baptist Church, 1979), "How to Shepherd" chapter.

time but it is one of the most productive investments which the
shepherd can make.[7]

The Second Year

Several changes transpired in the second year of training. In
August we began with a two-day retreat to a condominium
overlooking beautiful Lake Dillon.

The thrust of the year was discipleship. Course One and
Course Two of the Navigators' *2:7 Series** were used at each
training session. Class sessions required about thirty-minutes
preparation by trainees. Memory work and basic Bible study
were included. Basic principles of discipleship for spiritual
growth were stressed.

Monthly business meetings for the Board of Deacons and
Deaconesses were moved to the third Wednesday night of each
month. Previously, the meetings had been held on the third
Tuesday preceding the Wednesday night training class. That had
caused a strain on the families of shepherding teams, resulting
in absenteeism. The change was a welcome relief. Even though
the training program had one less class each month, the benefits of meeting together were retained. The morale of the corps
was heightened.

The Third Year

As the year began, the desire for spiritual renewal was a
primary concern. If a deeper work were to happen in the lives
of the lay shepherds, then prospects of a broad-based renewal
would be bright.

The book *Celebration of Discipline,* by Richard Foster, has

7. Eugene L. Stowe, *The Ministry of Shepherding* (Kansas City: Beacon Hill Press,
1976), p. 132.
  * *The 2:7 Series* (Colorado Springs: Navigators, 1973).

become the textbook of the year. One chapter a month is studied.

In September, "The Discipline of Meditation," was read and discussed by each husband-wife team. The chairman of Deacons and his wife, chairwoman of Deaconesses, were assigned a ninety-minute seminar on meditation. They read everything available to them on the subject.

On the night of their co-teaching, I sat in amazement. The presentation was very professional. It was the best teaching I had ever heard on the subject. I learned much about Christian meditation I had never heard before.

My wife and I were teaching an evening class, "Patterns for Christian Growth," at the seminary during this time. I asked Bill and Sharon Ward to bring a mini-version of their seminar to my class. The response of the class was electric. Hearing this lay-shepherding couple a second time, I marveled. The potential in lay people for spiritual teaching and leadership is often missed by over-committed professionals.

The next month we continued Foster's material on "The Discipline of Fasting." The couple assigned to the seminar read nearly thirty books and pamphlets on the subject of fasting. They experimented with fasting, using different methods and durations through the month. The deacon completed one five-day fast. This team, Bob and Bev Maitan, brought quality teaching that people would travel and pay to hear.

I asked this couple to bring a mini-version of their seminar to the evening service prior to the monthly observance of the Lord's Supper. Many in the congregation became interested and excited about fasting in their own lives.

The deacons and deaconesses declared a twenty-four-hour fast before their next monthly business meeting. This fast was climaxed with prayer and sharing around tables in the fireside room. Everyone celebrated with a soup and fruit banquet.

Fasting will play a significant part in the lives of our lay-shepherding teams. Hopefully the congregation will also be involved prior to meetings, focused on renewal, in the spring.

Richard Foster's chapter on the "Discipline of Simplicity" was used in December. In our affluent community, this emphasis was timely. The seminar by Bob and Jan Burnside was most convicting. They suggested strong alternatives to those in which most of us are living.

As I walked home that evening, I reflected on lay people teaching lay people to choose a simpler lifestyle. No preacher in the world could have handled the subject as effectively as the credible and sincere couple who had been our instructors.

The third year of training has featured Little Flock ministries plus a variety of other topics. The first Wednesday evening of the month has become a team night.

On the first Wednesday in October, the deacon-deaconess teams were assigned a home visit to a Little Flock household. Teams who had children brought them to midweek programs at church, then made the home visit. A written report was handed in at the next week's class.

On the first Wednesday night in November each team dropped off children before driving to a quiet place. Communication and prayer for each other was primary. The shepherds were instructed to conclude their evening in conversational prayer for members of their Little Flock.

The assignment for December was to leave the children at the midweek service. This gave the lay shepherd time to take his wife to a restaurant for dessert and coffee. There they planned their family activities for the holiday season.

In addition to team night, workshops with specialists were conducted once a month. These were designed to equip the lay shepherds to minister in practical ways.

One night in September was designated as a Study Night. Position papers had previously been distributed. I led the deacons and deaconesses in: A Scriptural Study on Divorce; How to Handle Divorce in the Church; How to Care for the Divorcing and Divorced Person.

In October a member who does financial planning presented a simple non-accounting plan for money management. This might be taught to Little Flock households willing to have help.

Still scheduled, is a seminar by a Christian doctor on enriching the intimate married life of mid-life couples.

Each year of lay-shepherd training has had strengths and weaknesses, but progress has been made. There is a general consensus that our handle on something good has just begun.

5

Lay Shepherds Develop
Their Style

The training sessions were designed to develop shepherd-leaders. Conformity in ministry was not intended. I believe that the Holy Spirit gives unique combinations of gifts to the servants He is equipping. Innovation and creativity were encouraged in the program. Different styles soon emerged becoming a trend which continues.

The training classes were designed to remind shepherds-in-training to keep God's purpose before them. The purpose must be identical with that of the Great Shepherd. The lay shepherd's role is not merely to "keep" people with Christ, but also to "develop" them for Christ's service. The objective is not maintaining people, it is nurturing them.

The functions of pastoral care are well-defined by Clebsch and Jaekle:

1. *Healing* is that function in which a representative Christian person helps a debilitated person to be restored to a condition of wholeness, on the assumption that this restoration achieves also a new level of spiritual insight and welfare.
2. *Sustaining* consists of helping a hurting person to endure and to transcend a circumstance in which restoration to his former condition or recuperation from his malady is

either impossible or so remote as to seem improbable . . . but it goes beyond mere resignation to affirmation as it attempts to achieve spiritual growth through endurance of unwanted, or harmful, or dangerous experiences.

3. The pastoral function of *guiding* consists of assisting perplexed persons to make confident choices between alternative courses of thought and action, when such choices are viewed as affecting the present and future state of the soul. . . .

4. The *reconciling* function seeks to re-establish broken relationships between man and fellow man and between man and God . . . reconciling employs two emphatic modes of operation which we call forgiveness and discipline.[1]

This last reconciliation of man with God's forgiveness, is the evangelistic responsibility of the shepherd. To use a metaphor from the world of sheep, this could be termed, "lambing." In Wyoming sheep ranching, lambing is the bottom line. The amount of profit is determined by the size of the lamb crop. Likewise, if pastoral care excludes the lambing/evangelistic process, it has degenerated into a maintenance ministry. The importance of lost sheep is discovered in the words of the Great Shepherd:

> Suppose one of you has a hundred sheep and loses one of them. Does he not leave the ninety-nine in the open country and go after the lost sheep until he finds it? . . . there is more rejoicing in heaven over one sinner who repents than over ninety-nine righteous persons who do not need to repent (Luke 15:4-7).

In the past, during the weekly training session, the first seven minutes have been used as a sharing time for lay shepherds. New activities and ministries were reported at that time. Occasionally, new ideas and approaches for effective shepherding

---

1. William A. Clebsch and Charles R. Jaekle, *Pastoral Care in Historical Perspective* (Englewood Cliffs: Prentice Hall, 1964), pp. 8-9.

have led into a natural brainstorming period. When this happened, the planned formal training was set aside for another week.

Periodically, "Report Forms of Little Flock Ministries by the Shepherding Teams" have been filled out and presented to the pastor-instructor.[2] The information that follows, describing the "on-the-job" training, is drawn from those reports.

The Social Life of the Church

The Sunday school classes had been the primary source of social contact, but an increasing number of people not in Sunday school were on the outside. The social and fellowship life of the church began to incline in the direction of the Little Flocks. This was a change.

Because the lay-shepherding program began officially on July 1, it was an ideal time of year for backyard barbecues, patio gatherings, and picnics. The fireside room of the church was booked regularly on Sunday after church for cooperative buffets of Little Flock gatherings.

This flurry of activity began to acquaint people with others in the church. Almost immediately, a warming trend was observed in the congregation. There was more visiting in the narthex of the church as people lingered longer after services. Reports drifted in that new friendships were being formed. Groups of couples were getting together outside the framework of the church.

One report described a Halloween party for families of a Little Flock in the fireside room.

There were forty in attendance at our Halloween party (dinner and games). The food for our covered dish dinner was terrific. We must have the best cooks of the entire church in our Little

---

2. Appendix 4, p. 96. See Sample "Report Form of Little Flock Ministries by the Shepherding Teams."

Flock. It was good for my wife and me to watch the families eating together. We learned a lot about them by just watching. Almost everyone was in a Halloween costume. A "best" costume was chosen from each group as men, women, boys and girls modeled their outfits. Our game time was for the entire family. Our Little Flock saw families together and began to get acquainted with each other as family units. As deacon and deaconess, we began to think of our Little Flock as whole families instead of just the adults.

Considerable creativity began to surface as the lay shepherds were encouraged to develop their own styles of ministry:

> Because pastors and elders recognize . . . the need for fellowship among the members of their congregations . . . an attempt will be made to encourage both formal and informal fellowship among the members. Creatively, they will think of ways in which to bring members of the congregation together to know one another *as human beings,* not merely as the persons who sit across the room in meetings.[3]

Prayer Meetings

Several Little Flocks held regular prayer meetings in which there was a sharing of requests and needs. Prayer was for those present as well as members who were absent.

One Little Flock held a Bible study in the home of its shepherding team alternate Tuesday evenings. A report from that group reads:

> We have been studying I Peter two nights a month on Tuesday evenings at our house. There are about ten to twelve who come on a regular basis. We've enjoyed it. And our meeting has provided a sharing in spiritual matters. My wife and I are beginning to feel that we are spiritually ministering to our people.

3. Adams, *The Pastoral Life,* p. 79.

The summer midweek ministry was assigned to the deacons, who coordinated with the Little Flock ministry. Three "prayer-share" meetings were held on Wednesday nights in the home of deacons and their wives. Four shepherding teams with their Little Flocks were assigned to each gathering. These teams met together on a rotating basis in the homes of the deacons assigned. Deacons took turns as leaders of the gatherings. Planning took into consideration vacations of those involved.

The summer midweek program proved to be an excellent on-the-job training experience. It gave the lay shepherds an opportunity to teach and lead prayer meetings. We concluded that it was the best midweek summer program the church has had.

Building Relationships

As relationships began to form between the shepherding teams and members, opportunities occurred for personal counseling. Sometimes this was a slow process. At one class session, a deacon asked,

> How can we get people to open up to us? We have one family on our list that's so private and reserved, we never get beyond "Hello! How are you?" When we have visited in the home, it gets uncomfortable and awkward. How do you get into spiritual matters?

On the spur of the moment, I suggested a technique I've used frequently. "I ask them, 'when I pray for you and for the members of your family, what can I pray for . . . how should I pray?'"

Two weeks later, during the Little Flock sharing period of the weekly class session, the same deacon raised his hand.

> The advice the pastor gave works like a top. We couldn't believe it. My wife and I visited our "closed-do-not-enter" family. It was

the same strained situation. Then, just before we were getting ready to leave, and I wanted to pray, I said: "We pray for each family in our Little Flock each week. When we pray for each member of your family, what should we pray for?" We couldn't believe what happened next. The woman began to tell about their teen-age daughter and the boyfriend who wasn't a good influence. They spoke of their concern about the junior high son who didn't want to go to church anymore. For the first time, we started to get into their lives. And all that happened when you gave us that simple question, Pastor!

Relationships that developed in the lay-shepherding teams helped people turn toward their lay shepherds for personal counsel.

As the senior pastor, I struggled with the shifting dependency of church members from me to others. I discovered something unhealthy in me that wanted people to need me more than anyone else. I grew up a little in the process. Because of the close involvement with the lay shepherds, the relinquishing process was easier.

I realized I was no longer the indispensable confidant in our congregation. Giving up this role for a man who delighted in being the pastor-shepherd marked the final translation from shepherd to ranch foreman.

Ministering to the Ill

During a six-month period, thirty-eight hospital calls were recorded by the shepherding teams. These provided relationships between the deacons, deaconesses and families under their care. Deaconesses often provided meals to the family at home during the hospitalization.

One deaconess' ministry is recorded in notes I jotted for my file.

One of our single women in her middle-aged years was hospitalized with a very painful kidney stone condition. Surgery was necessary, and her deaconess and I were together with her for prayer before surgery. I was impressed when the deaconess said to the woman, just before she was taken to surgery, "Now I want you to know that I'm going to be down in the waiting room while you're in surgery. I'll be praying for you there. When it's all over, I'll represent you as family when the surgeon comes out, and I'll tell you everything he says when you are conscious."

When I visited the recovering patient two days later, she said: "Pastor, you have no idea what it meant to a single person like me to hear someone say: 'I'm going to represent you as your family to the doctor.'" Tears came, and then she said: "I feel more a part of the family at Mission Hills than I did before."

Another ministry of caring for physical needs in the congregation is prayer for healing. When there is a need, someone will request a prayer service. The fifth chapter of James has been used as a guideline for praying for the sick.

> Is any one of you sick? He should call the elders of the church to pray over him and anoint him with oil in the name of the Lord. And the prayer offered in faith will make the sick person well; the Lord will raise him up (James 5:14-15).

Throughout the years God has honored the prayer of faith by deacons who have gathered to pray.

In the second year of lay shepherding, Alice Halbrook sustained severe eye damage in a youth activity. She and her husband, plus teen-age daughters, have had a ministry as youth sponsors. In a straw fight on a hay ride, straw struck her eye, detaching the outer layer.

After the injury, the layer would adhere temporarily then become detached. Many doctors and specialists were consulted. They agreed that no surgery could effect a permanent cure.

When detachment occurs the patient must have complete bed rest, with a patch over the affected eye and the other eye at complete rest. The patient must remain immobile for one week until attachment has taken place again.

This vivacious lady, with her effective youth ministry and Bible study to women, required one week out of four in bed for complete rest. She never knew when a detachment would occur. Planning anything was very tentative. Her life looked bleak.

Alice had an intense desire to be healed in order that He would be glorified. A deaconess told her that she believed God wanted to heal her. The inner witness grew.

There was fear that if she requested a prayer service for healing, and the Lord chose not to answer, the faith of young people would be shaken. Finally she was compelled to "ask."

Prayer services for healing are small, quiet gatherings including the ill, family members, deacons, and one or two pastoral staff persons. Alice asked if those who were such a part of her life could be present. Before the prayer service, she told them that if the Lord chose not to heal her she would love Him as much as if He did.

We gathered in the fireside room with fifty young people, family members and friends. I instructed participants in the promise of James 5. The deacons and I knelt around Alice who was kneeling at a chair. I anointed her with oil; we laid hands on her, praying earnestly with faith that He gave us.

These shepherds were ministering to a sheep with a physical need. The Great Shepherd extended His unseen hand through the hands of His undershepherds. "The prayer offered in faith will make the sick person well. . . . The prayer of a righteous man is powerful and effective" (James 5:15, 16).

Aware of His presence we arose, with an unusual calm measure of confidence, fringed with a question mark.

From that day Alice has not experienced another detachment of the top layer of that eye. She gives God the glory for His healing power. Hers is a vital life of touching many people for her Lord.

Evangelism

The shepherding ministry led to the salvation of some in the Little Flocks. One young member of the church had a wife who was not a Christian. She consented to attend church with her husband. The family, because of his membership, was assigned a deacon and deaconess in preretirement years. The deaconess nurtured the young wife with numerous expressions of care.

She reported an incident that might have thwarted her plan to bring the young wife into the Kingdom.

> We were received with a warm welcome. We chatted on for a short time about generalities, then said, "We have really come to share God's Word on this visit." The couple quickly found their Bibles, and we asked the young wife to read several salvation texts. . . . We suggested that she insert her name in the place of "whoever" in John 3:16. Tears flowed as she started to read this verse, and she quickly left the room. When she returned she apologized for crying. We answered, "The Lord loves a broken heart and a contrite spirit." Then we had a few words of encouragement to share the workbooks we left for a dual Bible study. The book by Rosalind Rinker on prayer was well received. We told them that the Lord's love was far greater than our love. My husband prayed for them.

Although this visit resulted in an emotional scene, the sowing of that seed of the gospel was rewarded in a harvest. Several months later the same deaconess wrote:

> The most thrilling incident in our Little Flock ministry for me was leading this dear little mother and wife to Christ in friendship evangelism. On the Sunday evening at the close of the Harold Carlson meeting many had gone forward to pray. The young husband was there, but I noticed his wife a couple of pews ahead of us standing alone. I slipped out of our pew and stood beside her and asked: "Would you like to pray?" She threw her arms around me, and we went forward and knelt at the altar, and she prayed to receive Christ . . . a little lamb come home.

Material Provision

A caring ministry for material needs has often been supplied through the program.

For years the church had received a deacon fund offering for the needy at the close of the monthly communion service. The offering was a few dollars to be used when dire circumstances arose. It was an unimportant matter in the life of the church. A Puritan work ethic guided our attitude. The smugness in most of our lives suggested, "God helps those who help themselves."

During the second year of the program something began to happen that changed this attitude. Each time the deacon offering was received, hundreds of dollars were counted. The money came from a broad base of the membership. The deacons and pastoral staff were dumbfounded.

Recently it was reported that over $2500 was in the deacon fund. Like Elijah's jug of oil, the more that was poured out, the more was replaced.

The question before the lay shepherds was thought provoking. "If Jesus were in our midst, whom would He help?"

Members were now viewed from a different perspective. We could see that the church had ministered to spiritual needs alone. The blindness referred to in the Book of James had been the indifferent, uncaring stance of the church.

> Suppose a brother or sister is without clothes and daily food. If one of you says to him, "Go, I wish you well; keep warm and well fed," but does nothing about his physical needs, what good is it?

Practices of the early New Testament church began to live again in the midst of this modern church.

> There were no needy persons among them. For from time to time those who owned lands or houses sold them, brought the money from the sales and put it at the apostles' feet, and it was distributed to anyone as he had need (Acts 4:34-35).

The eyes of the lay shepherds were opened to see material needs in numerous lives. Several unemployed in the congregation had suffering families. We developed a new dimension of shepherding care which has continued until the present.

The lay shepherd is in close contact with the families of his Little Flock. He and his wife seek to be sensitive, wise, and good stewards. When they become convinced that financial help should be extended in Christ's name, the deacon confers with the chairman of the Board of Deacons. They decide if a gift should be given in cash or substance (because I often have intimate knowledge, they ask me to ratify the decision).

The lay shepherd delivers the check or produce to the family. There is an opportunity for prayer. The result is appreciation from a family that has received a visit from a ministering angel. Often a deepened relationship between a lay shepherd and sheep results.

Some people in the Little Flocks are chronically in financial straits, due to poor management. To bail them out at every turn wouldn't be helpful. Lay shepherds soon discovered that defeat with money management results in spiritual defeat. Counsel in better financial management, practical suggestions for budgeting, and assistance in prioritizing long-term financial objectives has become another aspect of ministry.

A few vignettes of caring help to Little Flock members illustrate this program.

A widow with several children received her final tax notice, with the date the property would be listed for sale. The lay shepherd comforted the apprehensive family. After counsel with the Board of Deacons, payment of taxes was approved, and paid in full. That woman saw the love of Jesus through a church called by His name.

Two graduated seminary couples were eking out survival in an effort to begin a new Christian music ministry. Their cupboards were bare. Two hundred dollars for groceries was granted each couple. Their lay shepherd, a grocery distributor, took them to a wholesale warehouse to let them shop for themselves. After three years of scrimping in seminary plus a scantier year, the young women were ecstatic. One declared,

"It has been years since I've had so much fun. This is going to be the best Christmas ever at our house!"

A member whose mother had died had no money to travel for the funeral. An alert lay shepherd arranged for a check. He was greeted in the grieving home as though he were a visiting angel. He was.

When Christ is Lord in His church, He ministers materially through His people. Needs are met that arise in the lives of others in His care. Ronald Sider noted that God identified with the poor.

> . . . The Sovereign of the universe identifies with the weak and destitute . . . only in the incarnation can we begin dimly to perceive what God's identification with the weak, oppressed and poor really means. ". . . though he was rich," St. Paul says of our Lord Jesus, "yet for your sakes he became poor . . ." (II Cor. 8:9).
>
> He was born in a small, insignificant province of the Roman Empire. . . . His parents were too poor to bring the normal offering for purification. Instead of a lamb, they brought two pigeons to the temple. Jesus was a refugee (Matt. 2:13-15) and thus an immigrant in Galilee (Matt. 2:19-23). Since Jewish rabbis received no fees for their teaching, Jesus had no regular income during his public ministry. Nor did he have a home of his own. He warned an eager follower who promised to follow him everywhere, "Foxes have holes and birds of the air have nests, but the Son of Man has no place to lay his head" (Matt. 8:20). Jesus also sent out his disciples in extreme poverty (Luke 9:3; 10:4). . . . Only as we feel the presence of the incarnate God in the form of a poor Galilean can we begin to understand his words: "for I was hungry and you gave me food, I was thirsty and you gave me drink, . . . I was naked and you clothed me, . . . Truly, I say to you, as you did it to one of the least of these my brethren, you did it to me" (Matt. 25:35-40 RSV).[4]

4. Ronald J. Sider, *Rich Christians in an Age of Hunger* (Downers Grove: InterVarsity Press, 1977), p. 69.

Other Lay Ministries

The lay shepherds shared a collective ministry while pursuing and developing their own styles of pastoral care. One couple had an unusual telephone ministry with the members of their Little Flock. Another deaconess wrote notes of encouragement to the women she was shepherding. A lay shepherd had breakfast weekly at a local restaurant with different men from his shepherding group.

One deaconess, who had a special touch with teenagers, made Coke dates with different young people from her Flock. She ministered effectively in many lives. One shepherd recruited the men to work in building a room on the small house of an elderly widow in his group.

The innovation and creativity that surfaced became very practical pastoral care.

6

Care Catalyzes a Church

William Fletcher, in his doctrinal thesis, *A Caring Model for the Local Church,* observed:

> The place to begin is in the Christian community. Pastor and people must learn to care, first for one another, then for those outside. Helping a few to care is a start toward a caring community.[1]

The primary purpose of initiating the lay-shepherding program was to provide adequate pastoral care to everyone. Development of a sharing support group through Little Flocks was a second thought. To create a caring community was beyond my faith and vision. It is happening. Active love is contagious, growing with use. Our use of love to others allows us to receive an increasing measure from Him. This is aptly described in the song, "Pass It On."

> It only takes a spark to get a fire going, and soon all those around can warm up in its glowing.

> That's how it is with God's love, once you've experienced it: you spread His love to everyone, you want to pass it on.[2]

1. William M. Fletcher, *A Caring Model for the Local Church,* A Report of the Professional Project (Denver: Conservative Baptist Seminary, 1979), p. 2.
2. Kurt Kaiser, *Hymns for the Family of God,* "Pass It On" (Nashville: Paragon Associates, Inc., 1976), p. 641.

Lay shepherds and wives became instruments of Christ's compassion and care; they became catalysts in creating a climate. An entire congregation became a caring community.

Examples and illustrations are in order. In a public announcement, I asked those who had benefited to describe the ministry in writing. This resulted in numerous case histories of extended pastoral care. I share some of these.

Case Studies

A wife and the mother of four children, and a member of the church for many years has written:

"The most memorable time in my experience with real care was after our fire. Our house had been burning, and the firemen had just put it out. My neighbor, also a Mission Hills member, had called the prayer chain of the church.

"As I was stumbling through a tour of my blackened house, many of my church friends began to pour into my yard. The chairman of the Deacon Board was prompt to bring $100.00 from an emergency fund. I felt as if we were destitute.

"Caring Christians were saying: 'You're welcome to stay at our house tonight.' Others verbalized our thoughts: 'Where are you going to go?'

"Suddenly the voice of my deaconess took charge, almost ordered me: 'You will come to our house tonight.' Somehow she knew I couldn't make a decision. I needed a clear order!

"By the time we got there the house was loaded with bags of clothes, hangers of clothes, toys for the children, and money. Generosity and goodness came from all over the church. When I reflect back on that memorable day, my deaconess stands out!"

A lovely middle-aged woman who has undergone an unwanted divorce said:

"Going through this painful divorce has brought me to my knees in constant prayer for guidance. The one bright spot has been my ministering deacon and deaconess, George and Mary Jo Hockman.

"She has taken me to lunch many times. There she listened to my grieving and sorrowing with a concerned and loving heart. They invited me to be their guest for a weekend last summer at their cabin in the Rocky Mountain National Park. It was a weekend of sharing and caring in prayer. They were the most peaceful days; the only enjoyable days of the entire year.

"Their love just wrapped me up and made me glow for days afterward. Truly God has been good in sending to me His ministers of mercy."

A husband and father was hospitalized and underwent a very precarious surgery. His wife shared:

"We arrived home after the horrendous day of surgery. The three of us (mother and two teenage daughters) were weary and drained. Norma, our deaconess, had prepared and delivered to us the most lovely meal.

"It wasn't really necessary. The women of the house weren't hospitalized. We could have cooked. But it was just wonderful to sit down to a prepared meal after one of the worst days of our lives. We felt so loved, that someone cared to meet our needs at such a late hour."

A divorced mother who bore the entire financial brunt of rearing three small children told of a bright chapter in her life:

"It's so hard making ends meet around this house. With me in school, and the kids to provide for, there is never any extra left over.

"I couldn't believe it when my deaconess wanted to take me shopping for a new outfit for Christmas. She and her husband decided this was what they wanted to give to Jesus on His birthday. It meant so much to me. She has been a real help in discipling me since I accepted Christ.

"But to give me a gift for Jesus made me understand Christmas and Christianity a whole lot better."

Karen Kasch's brother Ron was diagnosed as being in the advanced stages of Hodgkin's disease. Ron was 23 years of age and not a Christian. Karen, in the early stages of pregnancy, traveled over 200 miles to visit him in the hospital. While there, she began to miscarry and was hospitalized. Karen's husband Russ phoned his deacon, Mel Anderson, for prayer. The roads were a solid sheet of ice, but the sound of Russ' voice on the phone was disturbed and frantic.

After prayer, Mel and Judy decided that they were needed during this difficult time. They drove the icy road to the hospital, where they ministered to Russ and Karen.

Then Mel visited Ron on another floor of the hospital. He led him to a saving knowledge of Christ. Ron's father commented on the difference. A lost sheep was brought into the fold.

Mel and Judy returned home after an exhausting and eventful day of shepherding.

A mother of a grown son and three teenage daughters described what shepherding care meant to her during the difficult days of divorce:

"On January 11, 1979, my small secure world fell apart when my husband chose to leave. I was suddenly faced with almost total responsibility for the support of three daughters and the bills of running a household. Three months before I had been involved in a serious multicar accident. I was facing a series of corrective surgeries.

"I felt very alone and helpless. My deacon and deaconess, Harry and Carol Schanker, as well as the shepherding group, ministered in a number of loving and practical ways.

"For a period of time, I had no income so that my meager savings were exhausted. I was able to provide only the least expensive soups, beans, and potatoes for my children.

"Our shepherding group, under the Schankers, made a point to open their homes for dinner. They included us in their families many times.

"I received anonymous financial help as well as food and assistance. Neither my daughters nor I ever felt like we were someone's 'responsibility'; only that we were loved and hurting family members.

"My lay shepherds loved us, prayed with us, hurt with us, and cried with us. They were as close as my telephone. When I did not call them, they called me.

"As a woman alone, with overwhelming family and financial responsibilities, I needed practical advice and constant encouragement. Help was needed in every area, from necessary home maintenance to college financing. Harry and Carol spent hours helping me reach career and financial decisions.

"Each time I was hospitalized, the Schankers were there. While hospitalized and during recovery, our shepherding group provided food, transportation, and extra tender loving care.

"The past three years have been a time of stress and turmoil, but also a time of great personal growth. The encouragement, love, and support of my shepherds, as well as other dear Christian friends, has kept my life together. I cannot read Matthew 25:35-40 without seeing the members of my 'family,' and my shepherds."

A deacon heard via the grapevine that the children of a black family in his Little Flock were hurt by peers' needless racial slurs and jokes. The deacon took their mother to lunch to hear the story.

He proceeded to initiate procedures in three youth groups to teach corrective measures. In one of the classes fellow students were visibly moved. The situation was corrected. Those involved learned lessons of sensitivity to the potential poison of the human tongue.

A divorced woman was plagued with breaking and entering of her house by her former mate. He knew which screens to take off. The windows were opened and things were missing from time to time. Two deacons spent an entire Saturday making the house secure. To that grateful woman's relief, there were no problems after that. Her home became a place of safety and refuge.

A young deaconess has felt the pressures of an unemployed husband. She wrote to the Board of Deaconesses what the chairwoman has meant to her as shepherdess.

"Our deacon and deaconess are Bill and Sharon Ward. We have never met more fantastic people. They are tremendous in their spiritual knowledge and practical insight. They are generous, thoughtful, kind, and available.

"I have never called Sharon with a problem that she didn't have time to help me. I've called her a lot this past year because I've been discouraged. She has taken hours to listen to me, to help me find answers. She doesn't just throw out some quick, nice-sounding, Christian platitude. She always takes time to share from her life and to find appropriate scripture for the need.

"Yet, I must add that she and Bill are so humble, human, and reachable. I never felt that they put themselves up as some great authority. They are quick to mention their weaknesses. We never felt that we alone had all the problems and areas of defeat. They gave us the impression that we are all in this together. We could help each other.

"Bill and Sharon have obviously meant so very much to us. They are exceptional. We, like the others, are seeking to do our best, but they have gone above and beyond the call of duty."

Ruth Herder was widowed four years ago. Her husband, Dean, was a leader and deacon of the church. Ruth was left with four children ranging from elementary to high school in age. She and her family exemplify a modern-day recognition that the care of widows and their children are the responsibility of the church. "Religion that God our Father accepts as pure and faultless is this: to look after orphans and widows in their distress . . ." (James 1:27). Ruth reflects on care extended to her and to the children through these years:

"As a widow, the male authority and influence of husband and father is missing. I look to God and His church (through the senior pastor and deacons) to care for my family both spiritually and in physical and material ways, too.

"Paul and Kaye Norlander have been our faithful deacon and deaconess. During the years my family was in their Little Flock, they helped us in so many different ways.

"I was so bewildered when it was necessary to change houses. They moved us, arranging for helpers, moving furniture and working long hours to get the job done.

"As I look back on it now, I think I just stood around being in the way. Without a husband, insecurity and fear sometimes overwhelm. My lay shepherds, both of them, gave much time, to meet and talk. Our family was invited to their home for ice cream and many social gatherings. They remembered us at Thanksgiving and Christmas with enough food for a feast.

"Paul gave endless financial advice. He spent hours going over my records, compiling back data, going to an attorney and a CPA, to file back income tax statements.

"When there were emergencies he arranged financial help through the deacon fund. He made minor car repairs, and then loaned me a car while mine was being fixed. He made home improvements and repairs when they were needed.

"A neighbor was drinking too much and threatened my family. We were all very afraid. I called the Norlanders who came immediately in response to the call.

"Others from our church family have helped in so many different ways. A number of families frequently give me money. Many have included us in their families. They warm our lives."

A further incident in this family's life warmed my heart. Laura, the second daughter, was having her first date. She planned for the big evening with detail and anticipation. With considerable sadness she shared with her mother one great regret. Her dad wouldn't be there to answer the door, meet her date, and wait with him before she made her grand entrance. They decided that "her" shepherd would be asked to stand in for her father. So Paul Norlander, lay shepherd, was Laura's father figure on that very important night.

Church Body—Catalyzed to Care

Ray Stedman described a quality of church life that was beginning to unfold at Mission Hills.

What is terribly missing is the experience of "body life"; that warm fellowship of Christian with Christian which the New Testament calls *koinonia,* and which was an essential part of early Christianity. The New Testament lays heavy emphasis upon the need for Christians to know each other, closely and intimately enough to be able to bear one another's burdens, confess faults one to another, rebuke, exhort, and admonish one another, minister to one another with the word and through song and prayer, and thus come to comprehend "with all saints" as Paul puts it, "What is the breadth and length and height and depth, and to know the love of Christ which surpasses knowledge" (Eph. 3:18-19, RSV).[3]

The shepherds seem to represent the heart of the body. They reflect God's compassion and mercy. When they care, life is pumped to the entire body. Care is not primarily an emotion, it is an act of compassion. The will decides to care.

It has been observed that a church eventually reflects the personality of a pastor. He gives leadership in subtle, indirect ways in addition to active leadership.

A very gregarious pastor resigned. His church was a spontaneous, uninhibited fellowship which had been formed under his leadership. The minister following him was a quiet-mannered scholar with reserved qualities.

I visited the church a year after the new leader had begun his ministry. The mood and atmospheric change was notable.

This is not as evident in a larger church where direct contact with the senior pastor is limited. Different staff members and lay leaders share in influencing congregational attitudes and personality.

In our church, qualities of compassion and concern were

3. Ray C. Stedman, *Body Life* (Glendale: Regal Books, 1972), p. 107.

translated through lay shepherds to the congregation. Shepherding care became the single most important thrust. Ministering care and concern became the hallmark of Christianity in our midst. We were becoming a caring church.

The apostle Paul emphasizes:

> If I speak in the tongues of men and of angels, but have not love, I am only a resounding gong or a clanging cymbal. If I have the gift of prophecy and can fathom all mysteries and all knowledge, and if I have a faith that can move mountains, but have not love, I am nothing. . . . the greatest of these is love (I Cor. 13).

As the senior pastor, my primary efforts were spent in pouring my shepherd's heart and life into laymen. We developed the program of shepherding so that all bases would be covered.

Lay shepherds became the catalysts of change to the congregation. They pumped love to the extremities of the church body.

Reviewing this progress, I recognize that the emphasis created a temporary lack of balance. Evangelism and Christian education did not receive sufficient emphasis.

In the third year of training, corrective measures are being taken to balance our emphases.

I remain convinced that Christ led our building of His church in this place. He desired to shepherd it into His love and care first. "God has poured out his love into our hearts by the Holy Spirit, whom he has given us" (Romans 5:5). Love was modeled by the leaders of His church. He lived and cared through their priesthood. The entire body was linked to His shepherding care.

After this basic process, He could develop His church as He planned. The first step needed to be established.

> A healthy church will care about the members of that congregation and respond to their needs. A healthy church will care about the turf, the place, the larger community where God has called it to be. In the act of healing, a healthy church will share its place with those in need. A healthy church will have an identity that is carried in the rhythm and pace of the congrega-

tion's life together. The identity they share comes from God, who touches them as a people in a place.[4]

A caring church becomes healthy. Christ's love finds in His people a prepared climate for His healing. It becomes the proper habitat for life by His Spirit to produce the health and wholeness of His love.

Christ's love through lay shepherds' care catalyzed His church. It became a healthy body ready to serve Him in evangelism, teaching, further shepherding, and salting its community.

4. Carl S. Dudley, *Making the Small Church Effective* (Nashville: Abingdon, 1978), pp. 119, 120.

7

Satisfied Sheep and Shepherd

Utopia has not arrived. The ultimate in a shepherding model is still to come off the assembly line at the Mission Hills Church. Nevertheless, many of us involved in the emphasis believe we have something good.

There is progress with improvement. Benefits that have extended to the congregation have helped the senior pastor. There is greater contentment among the sheep of the congregation. Better pastoral care is provided to the individual sheep of the entire flock.

The senior pastor appears not so burdened, more content and relaxed.

Satisfied Sheep

How can we measure the sense of well-being that care has provided in the congregation? Like sheep in green pastures and beside still waters, it is there. There is a sense of security and intimate belonging, even though total membership increases each month.

A new member, arriving at church without knowing anyone, exemplifies the satisfaction of many members. Charlotte Mather has written:

> Bob and Jan Burnside have shepherded me in a way I have never been helped before. I felt from the very first phone call that I had

65

true friends in Christ. They extend a warmth of love just as God sends the warmth of sunshine. Just knowing that Bob and Jan are there is a "warm fuzzy." I thank God for directing me to Mission Hills where we have the Shepherding Groups.

Satisfaction varies in the lives of different members. These accomplishments are noteworthy.

The lay-shepherding teams enjoy a meaningful service satisfaction. They are being used in a spiritual ministry that matters.

The spiritual nurturing care of human beings carries over into eternity. Scripture states that ministry is on Christ's behalf, in His stead. Many people on the lay-shepherding teams were involved previously in decision-making committees and boards. One deacon, executive of a large corporation, said:

I'm convinced that decision-making church boards are non-growth situations. I've always been placed on them in every church where we've been members. They bring out my carnal nature. Sometimes I wonder what percentage of decisions I've helped make on church boards and committees through the years have mattered at all in eternity.

Some lay people have gifts and talents for ministry which supersede those of their pastors. They wait to be challenged in meaningful services for their Lord and eternity. Unfortunately, a high percentage of today's clergy discriminate against lay status, rather than developing "tent-makers."

Throughout the years of our history, have we made a serious mistake as we transferred so much pastoral care to "the man of the cloth"? What would be the effect if we should change our thinking to consider our ordained pastor as "training minister" and consider our laymen as "the real ministers"?[1]

In the lay-shepherding ministry I saw people take priesthood into their lives. They served, functioning as pastors, in a distin-

1. Charles W. Shedd, *The Pastoral Ministry of Church Officers* (Atlanta: John Knox Press, 1974), p. 15.

guishing manner. The competency of lay persons in shepherding God's people far outshines the effectiveness of many professional ministers.

Lay shepherds reflect deep satisfaction in the nurturing, spiritual service.

Little Flock members express contentment because they are a cared-for people. Satisfaction of the sheep stems from two sources: the care of the lay shepherds and supporting friendship supplied by the Little Flock.

The care of the lay shepherds has far exceeded the senior pastor's earlier expectations. I was grasping, looking for assistance to benefit my overextended situation. I didn't perceive that lay people could minister in a shepherding capacity. They did, as records reveal. They extend comfort and encouragement to others whose troubles are similar.

One of the deacons was without employment for several months a few years ago. Now each Wednesday morning he invites several men of the church who are without jobs, as his guests at a restaurant. There at breakfast, that deacon has a ministry of encouragement and prayer.

Telephone calls, notes, home visits, and prayers have linked people to their lay shepherds. As the relationship blossoms, the satisfaction swells.

Several of the shepherding teams make "drop-in" calls to Little Flock members during the Christmas season. One deacon and deaconess delivered miniature poinsettia plants; another couple gave Christmas tree ornaments with Scripture on them; another brought small decorative holly plants to each household; others gave plates of Christmas cookies and candies. Satisfaction, contentment, and reciprocal love result from such care.

The Little Flock is designed to be a small church family. At its best it functions in this manner. When there is illness, the Little Flock rallies to support and assist. Presently a member of the church is home as a terminal patient. Church members take turns spending each night with the patient.

During hospitalization and home recovery, the Little Flock

members assist with food, transportation, lawn cutting, snow shovelling, and child care.

A list of support and care is endless. The primary contribution is not services rendered, which may be bought. It is the friendship extended with assistance. There is a satisfaction in belonging.

Presently, a young father of four small sons is hospitalized for tests. Malignancy is feared. The concern and anxiety of his little church family could be no greater if there were a close blood relationship.

The suburbs can be a very lonely place to live. Large churches are often a collection of strangers. Such a community needs "the essential character of the small church, an intimacy, the capacity to know and care about others."[2]

A Sane Overseeing Shepherd

Compare the condition of the senior pastor, as he appeared initially, contrasted to his state in the epilogue.

Back in 1976, I was beginning to "want out," but was hemmed in. My wife was happy in the church. Her unofficial role, as assistant pastor in earlier years, had diminished. The church had grown and acquired a multiple staff.

Church members gave every indication that they were responding to my ministry and expecting a long pastorate. Common sense indicated that closing my ministry would be traumatic for the church, perhaps resulting in instability and loss.

I was tired inside. The joy of ministry was fading. Listed in my prayer book of those days, was the request: "renew my call; give me a new vision of ministry."

At that moment I wanted release from the responsibility, which had become too much. I was convinced that I had activated the Peter Principle. I was inadequate to handle the situa-

2. Dudley, "Membership Growth, The Impossible Necessity."

tion of my own making. This overextended pastor would have welcomed a call to a less demanding ministry.

A crisis was mounting. I needed to understand and apply the advice of Jethro to his son-in-law Moses.

Moses' father-in-law replied, "What you are doing is not good. You and these people who come to you will only wear yourselves out. The work is too heavy for you; you cannot handle it alone. Listen now to me and I will give you some advice, and may God be with you. You must be the people's representative before God and bring their disputes to him. Teach them the decrees and laws, and show them the way to live and the duties they are to perform. But select capable men from all the people—men who fear God, trustworthy men who hate dishonest gain—and appoint them as officials over thousands, hundreds, fifties and tens. Have them serve as judges for the people at all times, but have them bring every difficult case to you; the simple cases they can decide themselves. That will make your load lighter, because they will share it with you. If you do this and God so commands, you will be able to stand the strain, and all these people will go home satisfied" (Exod. 18:17-23).

This Scripture portion projected a principle which renewed one pastor's life in the twentieth century. A modern day Moses, of Denver, Colorado, can declare the wisdom of Jethro's counsel.

Sharing the task of shepherding with a corps of lay people brought sanity and satisfaction in several ways.

I multiplied myself into thirty-six other lives by sharing the responsibility of shepherding 700 people with them.

It wasn't as easy as it sounds. In the initial stages of planning the program and writing the training manual, plus preparing lessons for each week's session, I wondered if I had made a mistake.

Adding this expenditure of time and effort to an overextended life appeared to be foolhardy. It was necessary to keep my long-range objective before me. At times of faltering, God's spirit gave a clear vision of what it would be like "out there."

Several months into the program small encouragements

came, but the possibility of a major shift did not occur until the second year. To my surprise, I had to decide again whether I really wanted to relinquish my exclusive rights to shepherding the body.

The real sharing and multiplying began when a part of myself was given up. My life merged with my lay-shepherd partners. Since then, commendable and competent shepherding gives me deep personal satisfaction.

This is a higher quality than a sound investment of time and energy. My life is bound into the lives of those who share this ministry with me. I discover my style of shepherding extending through them.

Thirty-six people, trained, assigned, and committed to share shepherding are making an impact, superior to my one-man ministry of several years ago.

It is no surprise that a corps of shepherds is producing more competent pastoral care than when it was under a one-man ministry.

That knowledge enables me to rest better nights. It lifts a considerable strain and stress from my daylight hours as well.

There is a special relationship between the lay shepherds and myself that I find most satisfying. They have become my principal support group, even though I have a staff of six professionally trained people. The lay shepherds are my friends; an affinity exists in our lives. Our association, based on ministry and not decision-making, has resulted in a camaraderie that has been a zenith in my relational experiences.

This is in contrast to the feeling that prevails between myself and my colleagues on our pastoral staff. While we have worked well together and have excellent rapport, because most of them are younger, I have been the father figure or the "boss," even in the lighter, more social times.

The Chairman of the Board of Deacons meets me early each Wednesday morning. We've laughed, cried, and prayed together. I've shared my deepest thoughts, greatest anxieties, and self-centered hurts with him. He has seen me at the throne room and under a juniper tree. This man is my friend, confidant, and partner. Other deacons with whom I've worked and shared through these years have linked their lives with mine. They see the best and worst side of their shepherding pastor. They accept me anyway.

Many pastors speak of the pastorate as a lonely life. I do not. Partnership in the lay-shepherding ministry has become my support group.

Sanity and ministry satisfaction did not come in freeing up time for a magnitude of ministerial tasks. It came when sensing that personal gifts arc tracking well, I have realized that I will not be a superstar according to ministerial standards. I know that the congregation needs a leader who as a man of God shepherds other shepherds.

The Lord has reassigned me. I've been promoted to a new job on the same ranch. He has made a ranch foreman out of a shepherd.

8

Shepherding:
A Scriptural Perspective

The Christian faith, which I embrace, originates in revelation. Revelation comes to man in two forms: natural and supernatural. Because all people are spiritually blind, natural revelation fails to give a reliable knowledge of spiritual things.

To offset this lack of knowledge, God discloses Himself in supernatural revelation. This is inscripturated in the Bible. This God-breathed revelation is infallible. It is wholly trustworthy in matters of history and doctrine.

> Nor do we need to do more than remind ourselves that this attitude of entire trust in every word of the scriptures has been characteristic of the people of God from the very foundation of the church. Christendom has always reposed upon the belief that the utterances of this book are properly oracles of God.[1]

The man who shepherds in the manner God intended comes to God's Word for truth and instruction. In the Old Testament Yahweh is pictured as the Shepherd of Israel. In the New Testament Jesus describes Himself as the Good Shepherd. He trained His apostles to be shepherds of people. Apostles then, taught and trained congregational leaders, overseers, elders and deacons,

---

1. Benjamin B. Warfield, *The Inspiration and Authority of the Bible* (Philadelphia: The Presbyterian and Reformed Publishing Co., 1948), p. 107.

in the leadership, feeding, and care of the people of the New Testament church.

Yahweh as the Shepherd of Israel

The Old Testament pictures Yahweh as the Shepherd of Israel. The first Old Testament reference to Yahweh as a shepherd is Jacob's blessing for the sons of Joseph:

> May the God before whom my fathers Abraham and Isaac walked, the God who has been my Shepherd all my life to this day, the Angel who has delivered me from all harm—may he bless these boys (Gen. 48:15-16).

The Old Testament is replete with this image of Yahweh.

> In the Old Testament the description of Yahweh as the Shepherd of Israel is ancient usage, but the surprising paucity of references in which the title is used of Yahweh shows that this is not just a formal divine prediction. The application of the shepherd image to Yahweh is embedded in the living piety of Israel.[2]

The psalmist David had been a shepherd and became known as the "Shepherd King" of Israel. He authored the twenty-third Psalm which begins, "The LORD is my shepherd." The Lord who dominates the psalm is Yahweh, the Lord God of Israel.

Yahweh, as the God who led Israel out of Egypt, is addressed in the metaphor of shepherd in Psalm 80:1-2.

> Hear us, O Shepherd of Israel, you who lead Joseph like a flock; you who sit enthroned between the cherubim, shine forth before Ephraim, Benjamin and Manasseh. Awaken your might; come and save us.

The prophets write of the covenantal relationship in pastoral terms.

---

2. Kittel and Friedrich, *Theological Dictionary of the New Testament*, 4:487.

For this is what the Sovereign LORD says: I myself will search for my sheep and look after them. As a shepherd looks after his scattered flock when he is with them, so will I look after my sheep. I will rescue them from all the places where they were scattered on a day of clouds and darkness (Ezek. 34:11).

Yahweh was pictured in the metaphor of a human shepherd. However, the Hebrew rightfully thought of God as Spirit. The concept of Yahweh the shepherd was sometimes difficult to understand. Because Yahweh's representative shepherds failed to be good shepherds, they tarnished the image.

The Sovereign Lord spoke of such shepherds through Ezekiel, "Woe to the shepherds of Israel who only take care of themselves! Should not shepherds take care of the flock?" (Ezek. 34:2).

Charles Jefferson aptly describes the period prior to the Good Shepherd's coming.

But while there was a good shepherd in the skies, there was no good shepherd on the earth. All the shepherds of Israel, one after another, proved disappointing. They did not do their duty. They failed to feed the flock. They did not wisely guide it. They could not save it. But the Hebrew heart did not despair. It dared to dream of an ideal shepherd who would surely come. A Messiah had been promised, and he would be a shepherd. He would guide and feed and save the sheep.[3]

Yahweh caring for his sheep comes into focus in the progressive revelation of Scripture. In the New Testament Jesus presents Himself as The Good Shepherd.

Jesus as the Good Shepherd

The Son of God in human form came describing Himself as The Good Shepherd (John 10:11-18):

3. Jefferson, *The Minister As Shepherd*, p. 15.

The name "pastoral" is a uniquely Christian term that expresses a
fundamental concept that is deeply imbedded in every Biblical
portrayal of Christian ministry. The term refers to a rich scripture figure that finds its beginning and end in God. He, who is
the "Shepherd of Israel" (Psalm 80:1), ultimately demonstrated
the meaning of His covenantal love as The Great Shepherd of the
sheep by giving His life for them.[4]

The term *shepherd* seemed to come into its own when Jesus
appeared. He took the title on Himself. Jesus never called Himself a priest, a preacher, a bishop, or an elder, but apparently
liked to think of Himself as a shepherd.

He presented Himself as a good shepherd, one who really
cared for His sheep, in contrast to "hired hands" who cared
nothing. When the wolf came, the hired hand abandoned the
sheep and ran away. Jesus declared, "I am the good shepherd; I
know my sheep and my sheep know me . . . and I lay down my
life for the sheep" (John 10:14-15).

The ministry of Jesus embodied relationship to others by
shepherding. Wherever He went, people needed His kind of
care:

In the sixth chapter of Mark's gospel we find Him taking a day off
with His disciples. Nobody needed it more than He. But when
they reached their destination, a quiet desert retreat, they found
it no longer private, but overrun with people. People who
wouldn't let well enough alone. People so rude and inconsider-
ate that they didn't even apologize for aborting His plans for
much needed rest and relaxation. Certainly He would have been
justified in telling them to "get lost!" After all, enough is enough.
But He didn't. He couldn't. "And Jesus, when he came out, saw
much people, and was moved with compassion toward them,
because they were as sheep not having a shepherd: and he began
to teach them many things" (Mark 6:34, KJV).[5]

4. Adams, *The Pastoral Life*, p. 5.
5. Eugene L. Stowe, *The Ministry of Shepherding* (Kansas City: Beacon Hill Press,
1976), p. 19.

Jesus, as the Shepherd-Savior, has an unusual appeal. Thousands who have lived a lifetime removed from contact with sheep are drawn into the metaphor. Jesus told of the shepherd searching for the one lost sheep. People identify with that lost sheep.

There is a personal appeal in a hymn that is sung around the world.

> Savior, like a shepherd lead us,
> Much we need thy tender care;
> In thy pleasant pastures feed us;
> For our use thy folds prepare.[6]

Apostles as Shepherds

Jesus was aware of the need to prepare shepherds and workers.

When he saw the crowds, he had compassion on them, because they were harassed and helpless, like sheep without a shepherd. Then he said to his disciples, "The harvest is plentiful but the workers are few. Ask the Lord of the harvest, therefore, to send out workers into his harvest field" (Matt. 9:36-38).

During His earthly ministry Jesus commissioned twelve disciples for a special role. Mark says, "He appointed twelve— designating them apostles—that they might be with him and that he might send them out to preach and to have authority to drive out demons" (Mark 3:14-15).

The Twelve performed three functions, while they were with Jesus. They were with Him as companions until His death. The second function was preaching. Mark 6:12 uses the term *keryssein,* which is translated, "to preach" or "to proclaim." But Mark

---

6. Dorothy A. Thrupp, "Savior, Like a Shepherd Lead Us," *Worship and Service Hymnal* (Chicago: Hope Publishing Co., 1960), p. 500.

6:30 says, "The apostles gathered around Jesus and reported to him all they had done and taught (*edidaxan*)."

The postresurrection teaching ministry, including the apostles' doctrine (Acts 2:42), can be traced back to this beginning. The third function was to exercise authority over evil spirits (Mark 6:7). Mark 6:13 adds to that authority over evil spirits, anointing and healing of sick people.

Each function of preaching and teaching, and delivery from satanic oppression with healing, is rudimental to shepherding people in the name of Christ.

Jefferson refers to the poignant scene by the seaside where Jesus restored His apostle, Simon Peter.

> The history of the church began with Jesus saying to the leader who is to head the work of discipling the nations: "I am a shepherd, be thou a shepherd, too."

Testing Simon Peter's love, Jesus said:

> "Feed my lambs . . .
> Take care of my sheep . . .
> Feed my sheep . . ." (John 21:15-17).[7]

Following Christ's death, resurrection, and ascension, the leading persons among Christ's followers were the apostles. There were eleven following the betrayal and demise of Judas Iscariot. Matthias was chosen to complete the Twelve. During replacement Peter, in Acts 1:20, said in reference to Judas Iscariot, "May another take his place of leadership (*episkope*)."

If there were no other evidence, this statement substantiates the apostles as shepherds.

> To carry on the work of an overseer (*episkopos*, "bishop") does not mean to do the work of any sort of overseer in general, but in the New Testament it always carries the idea of overseeing *as*

7. Jefferson, *The Minister as Shepherd*, p. 10.

a shepherd. It involves the all-embracing oversight required by the descriptions of such in Psalm 23, John 10 and elsewhere.[8]

The importance of the twelve apostles in the formative stages of the church in Jerusalem can hardly be overstated. In the truest sense they were the shepherds of the small growing movement.

Undoubtedly the first apostolic men of the primitive community also governed that community, possessed special honor within it, and took decision concerning it. The vital meaning of Christian witness, embracing as it does the whole of life, would certainly lead us to assume this, and Paul and Luke confirm it.[9]

A crucial part of shepherding in the formative church's existence was the teaching, feeding ministry by the apostles.

Those who accepted his message were baptized, and about three thousand were added to their number that day. They devoted themselves to the apostles' teaching and to the fellowship, to the breaking of bread and to prayer (Acts 2:41-42).

So the Twelve gathered all the disciples together and said, "It would not be right for us to neglect the ministry of the word of God in order to wait on tables. Brothers, choose seven men from among you who are known to be full of the Spirit and wisdom. We will turn this responsibility over to them and will give our attention to prayer and the ministry of the word" (Acts 6:2-4).

At the church in Jerusalem, Peter emerged as the natural leader of the community. Peter with the apostles ruled and governed the affairs of the primitive Christian community. The Twelve taught the "teaching of the apostles"; they received gifts to be distributed in the community of believers, and they pro-

8. Adams, *The Pastoral Life,* p. 8.
9. Hans von Campenhausen, *Ecclesiastical Authority and Spiritual Power* (Stanford: Stanford University Press, 1969), p. 27.

vided leadership. Outside Jerusalem they assisted by sending Peter and John to Samaria to a newly-forming church.

In the term *apostle* (New Testament usage) there is a distinction between the Twelve and general use of the term.

> In fact, for Paul "apostles" are not only the twelve: Andronicus and Junias are "outstanding among the apostles" (Rom. 16:7), where "the apostles" already appear as a category of office of the community (I Cor. 12:28f; Eph. 2:20; 4:11). . . . In other words, around 55 A.D. there already were many "apostles" who were not of the twelve. This notion of apostle (one not of the twelve) certainly applies to Paul himself and, very likely to many other unspecified "apostles."[10]

Paul emerges as a particular apostle. While most persons apart from the Twelve are referred to as apostles in the functional sense alone, this is not true of Paul. Though he was not one of the Twelve, Scripture indicates he had a unique calling. He was the apostle to proclaim the gospel to the Gentiles, Christ's particular representative to the non-Jew.

> But when God, who set me apart from birth and called me by his grace, was pleased to reveal his Son in me so that I might preach him among the Gentiles, I did not consult any man, nor did I go up to Jerusalem to see those who were apostles before I was, but I went immediately into Arabia and later returned to Damascus (Gal. 1:15-17).

Paul became an overseeing shepherd to all the churches he established in Gentile territory:

> Paul knows that his congregations need him, and cannot as yet do without him, and his disquiet increases when alien, destructive influences seek to intrude between him and his people. Moreover, the nature of his relationship with them seems to be such that there is no reason why it need come to an end. . . . The

10. Miguens, *Church Ministries in New Testament Times*, p. 25.

relationship is thus a permanent and reciprocal one, which will reach its term only at the last day.[11]

The tender care of the apostles in the first-century church is graphically depicted by the apostle Paul.

> As apostles of Christ we could have been a burden to you, but we were gentle among you, like a mother caring for her little children. We loved you so much that we were delighted to share with you not only the gospel of God but our lives as well, because you had become so dear to us (I Thess. 2:7-8).

Overseers and Elders as Shepherds

The Greek word *episkopos* means overseer or bishop. In I Peter 2:25 Christ Himself is called *episkopos*. The conception of Good Shepherd and overseer of His church are closely related.

> In general, the terms ποιμαίνεω and ἐπισκοπειν were closely linked in describing the work of the shepherd. . . . The phrase "Shepherd and bishop of your souls" carries within it all that is said by Greek speaking Gentiles and Jews about God as ἐπίσκοπος. As suggested by the context, which points us to the deepest mysteries of salvation history, ἐπίσκοπος is thus a title of majesty ascribed to Jesus in His work in relation to the community.[12]

The term *episkopos* was applied to the leaders in the first-century church. They were overseeing or supervising in Christ's place. Usage in early history described function as a supervising leader rather than a fixed office. Paul addressed the elders of the Ephesian church telling them that God had made them overseers.

> Guard yourselves and all the flock of which the Holy Spirit has made you overseers. Be shepherds of the church of God, which he bought with his own blood (Acts 20:28).

11. von Campenhausen, *Ecclesiastical Authority and Spiritual Power*, pp. 44, 45.
12. Kittel and Friedrich, *Theological Dictionary of the New Testament*, 2:615.

The first Christian use of *episkopos* was in the Hellenistic churches located in Gentile territory. A secular use of the term had origins in Greek culture. Quite naturally the word was adapted to the overseers and supervisors of Christian churches in that setting. Prior to Paul's pastoral letters several leaders in each congregation were recognized and addressed as bishops and overseers.

Initially, several bishops or overseers shared the responsibility of leadership in each church. There is the suggestion in Paul's pastoral letter to Timothy, in I Timothy 3:2, that the overseer was a single position in that local church. Responsibilities of overseers were similar to those of pastors in the twentieth century.

The Greek word *presbyteros* means elder. The original meaning had reference to men with maturity and spiritual experience. The Jews traced the beginning of eldership back to the time of Moses. When the burden of leadership became too heavy to bear, seventy "elders" were gifted with the Spirit which had rested exclusively on Moses. After that time eldership was incorporated into Jewish tradition becoming a permanent fixture in the Hebrew religious community. The primitive Christian churches organized themselves along Judaistic lines that they had always known.

> The system of elders is therefore probably of Judaeo-Christian origin, just as bishops and deacons were at first at home only in Gentile Christian congregations.[13]

Though the term *presbyteros* was carried over from the Jewish community, the role of Christian elders was quite different from the very beginning.

There were similarities. Elders of the Christian community had charge of the financial administration of each church. It was to the local elders that Paul and Barnabas delivered money sent to relieve the poor brothers of Jerusalem during the famine.

---

13. von Campenhausen, *Ecclesiastical Authority and Spiritual Power,* p. 77.

Jewish elders had exercised order and discipline over members of their synagogue. Christian elders comprised the council of the Judaeo-Christian church.

> They, together with the apostles, are the representatives of the local community of Jerusalem to receive envoys from other communities (Acts 15:4); they, together with the apostles, form the supreme court of appeals on questions concerning doctrine and, as a result, practical life among Christians (Acts 15:2, 6, 22, 23; 16:4); in Acts 21:18 they appear as the senate of only one leader, James.[14]

There are marked dissimilarities too. Personal compassion and care were unknown among the Jewish elders. This is the pastoral aspect alluded to by James, prominent elder in the Jerusalem Christian community. In James 5:13-16, James gave shepherding instruction for his elders. In sickness the elders were to anoint with oil "in the name of the Lord" for restoration. James implies that elders were to act as confessors and intercessors. They had a responsibility not only for those ailing physically, but also for the spiritually weak.

The elders, ministering "in the name of the Lord," were continuing the shepherding ministry of Jesus. He was using their hands to touch the helpless and the harassed.

There was another marked difference between elders of the Jewish synagogues and those of Christian assemblies. Elders of the synagogue were administrators, not preachers or teachers.

> The elders were the administrators of the synagogue; they did not preach, but they saw to the good government and order of the synagogue and then exercised discipline over its members.[15]

The elders of the church were responsible for sound doctrine. This was apparent, as dangers to the new movement increased.

14. Miguens, *Church Ministries in New Testament Times,* p. 39.

15. William Barclay, *The Letters of James and Peter* (Philadelphia: Westminster Press, 1977), p. 263.

In the twentieth chapter of Acts, Paul arranged for the elders of Ephesus to meet him in Miletus. The apostle's primary concern was a developing crisis with reference to the doctrine of unadulterated truth. Paul charged the elders to watch lest the flock be led astray and destroyed.

> Guard yourselves and all the flock of which the Holy Spirit has made you overseers. Be shepherds of the church of God, which he bought with his own blood. I know that after I leave, savage wolves will come in among you and will not spare the flock. Even from your own number men will arise and distort the truth in order to draw away disciples after them. So be on your guard! (Acts 20:28-31).

Function of overseers in Hellenistic territories and elders in the Judaeo community was the same. The terms applied were the difference. Prior to the council in Jerusalem, designations and distinctions of Hellenistic or Jewish extraction are fairly easy to differentiate. Then the congregations mingled and interpenetrated so that the terms *elder-presbyteros,* and *overseer-episkopos,* were used synonymously and interchangeably.

In their study of organizational life, pastoral epistles offered the last word of the New Testament period. The ambiguity of the term *elder* and *overseer* continued.

In the first letter to Timothy, offices of overseer and deacon appear to be highly developed. The apostle went into detail about necessary qualifications for the offices of overseer and deacon. Two qualities are noteworthy in the I Timothy 3 passage. The overseer is presented in the singular (elsewhere elders and overseers have been regarded as several in number). The second matter is that the term *elder* is conspicuous by its absence. It seems that it has been assimilated and incorporated into the office of overseer.

Another pastoral epistle penned by Paul from the same period of his ministry is addressed to Titus. Paul instructs Titus to appoint elders in every town. In that letter, Titus 1:7, the apostle identifies the work of an appointed elder as an overseer entrusted with God's work. In that same passage Paul elaborates on the feeding shepherd dispensing God's truth.

> He must hold firmly to the trustworthy message as it has been taught, so that he can encourage others by sound doctrine and refute those who oppose it (Titus 1:9).

Whatever the designation, elder or overseer, these leaders were to display the same leadership among the flock that Jesus would. By His Spirit He empowered elders and overseers who ministered with His shepherd heart "in His name."

Deacons as Shepherds

The English word *deacon* comes from the Greek noun *diakonos* which occurs twenty-eight times in the New Testament. The related feminine noun *diakonia* occurs thirty-two times. The noun form means waiter, servant, helper, and minister. The verb *diakoneo* meaning to wait on tables, serve, and minister, is used thirty-nine times in the New Testament.

Many of these New Testament references are not in relationship to the role of a deacon in a church. Most were directed to servants' work, waiting on tables, helping or serving other persons. This is what the word *diakonos* meant. Society viewed it as a lowly demeaning job, humiliating to the person performing the service.

Jesus took those humiliating connotations and lifted them, declaring that it was the highest way to live. He spoke of Himself in this language. Mark 10:45 might be translated, "For even the son of man did not come to be deaconed, but to deacon, and to give his life as a ransom for many."

It was to this style of living that Jesus called His disciples. The essence of the disciple life was to serve and minister to others.

Each believer, indwelt by the Spirit of Christ, has the heart of a shepherd. Having the heart of a servant-deacon is the essence of Jesus, so every believer is directed in Christ's stead.

The church selects members to be its Board of Deacons. This never cancels the responsibility of every Christian to live the servant life.

The seven men of Acts 6:1-6 were chosen like the twentieth-century deacon to provide leadership, care, and concern. The "harassed and helpless, like sheep without a shepherd" of Jesus' day, were in the same category as people today.

Those of Acts 6 have been viewed as the first group of deacons, even if unnamed in Scripture. Some scholars have made an issue of the absence of the term. Regardless of the absence, the function of deacon is evident.

> It should be emphasized, however, that in all later centuries this passage in Acts 6 has done more to shape the idea men form about deacons than any other Biblical passage.[16]

In Philippians 1:1, Paul mentioned two groups of leaders in the church in Phillipi. One is comprised of bishops or overseers. They were the officers governing and leading the local church. The other group contained deacons who were the helpful servants and ministers. These, too, were officers and leaders of the local church.

In I Timothy 3:1-13, Paul refers to the same two kinds of officials in the local church. In this passage the office of bishop is singular. Scholars suggest that one overseer was already established practice, becoming fully developed in the patristic period. It appears that the overseer Paul describes has qualifications similar to pastor of a local contemporary church.

In contrast, the group of deacons was plural. The passage references a list of personal qualities for deacon, but gives no description of the duties.

> Amazingly little is said as to their duties. It is from Acts 6, not from Philippians 1:1 or I Timothy 3:8-13 that the church has

---

16. Floyd V. Filson, "Lay Ordination" (Chicago: 1964), p. 6. (Mimeographed.)

taken the conception of the deacon as combining duties in relief work, preaching, and administering the sacraments.[17]

As the church moved into the patristic period, through the first two decades of the second century, the function of the church offices crystallized. A fixed order became more pronounced. Because there were no church buildings, groups of Christians met in homes and other available places. The bishop became leader of all small congregations throughout each city.

The Pauline letters addressed to specific churches were read by numerous small congregations of the church in that city. These small groups needed to express their unity. This was accomplished through the overseeing bishop.

The three offices, bishop, elders, and deacons, were clearly delineated in the patristic writings of the second century. Ignatius of Antioch wrote that these three offices were a necessary essential structure in the church.

> You should honor all the deacons like Jesus Christ, the bishop like the image of the Father, and the elders as the council of God and the gathering of the apostles. Without these one cannot talk of the church (Trall. 3:1).[18]

Elders and deacons of each congregation became leaders under authority of their local overseer or bishop. The elders became leaders, administrators, and teachers of the small congregations. There was merely a short step between this and the developing priesthood.

> This brought the deacons into touch with the bishop. His concern for the unity of the church and for the meeting of human need led to close ties between the bishop and the deacons. If, as seems to have been the case, the common meals of the church were a means of giving relief to needy Christians, and the deacons had duties in connection with those common meals, and if

17. Ibid., p. 7.
18. Lukas Vischer, "The Problem of the Diaconate" (Faith & Order Commission, World Council of Churches, July, 1963), p. 5. (Mimeographed.)

those common meals recalled Jesus' meals with his disciples and
especially his Last Supper with them, it can be seen that this
would further close ties of the deacon with the bishop, who
would be in charge of the sacraments.[19]

The next historic development for the deacon was to view
his office as the first advancement to the priesthood. Two things
had happened. The deacon was no longer a lay person, in our
present use of that term. Of greater gravity was the movement
away from the care-giving function of the office. The deacon's
duties came to be preparing for the priesthood lying ahead for
him. The attending-to-needs function lost its importance as a
vital role while the deacon worked on eligibility to become
a priest. Liturgical and administrative functions became pre-
eminent.

Unfortunately this care-giving work of today's deacon is still
minimal in function. The role has been reduced to Thanksgiving
baskets, and special relief when the Department of Welfare is
slow or unable to act.

There is a trend in baptistic and evangelical churches to
fortify the Board of Elders. This minimizes the Board of Deacons
or reduces it to trustee status. History indicates that churches
and movements following this pattern almost inevitably have a
strong Board of Elders. They govern and administer the business affairs of the church while the overseeing of souls is
neglected.

The term *servant-diakonos,* assures an attitude which will
"not lord it over those entrusted to you" (I Peter 5:3):

It is interesting to notice that this word "deacon," which from
the first has implied some form of leadership, does not carry the
connotation of power and prominence. This simple, ordinary
word for service is used to speak of Christ's service to men and
of the service owed one who is a Christian to God, to Christ, and
to his fellows. In this way the New Testament clarifies the pastoral character which should be the mark of the church, corpo-

---

19. Floyd V. Filson, "Lay Ordination" (Chicago: 1964), p. 10. (Mimeographed.)

rately as a total people of God, and individually, both in places of leadership and in the private responsibility one bears in life. This concept of service makes all Christian leaders servants of servants, supporting them, leading, counselling, and instructing them in their ministries.[20]

There is much of the shepherd's caring compassion in a deacon's ministry. If his care-giving ministry could be continued with spiritual guidance, then the quality of shepherding helpless harassed people would become the shepherding Jesus intended.

The term *servant-diakonos* has potential in today's contemporary church.

The Greek language offered many designations from personal or cultic associations for the Church's office, but instead of accepting these the Church developed a new designation which was common to neither the Jewish nor the Hellenistic environment, διακονία "service" or διακονεῖν "to serve." Since this term occurs in the Synoptic as well as the Pauline terminology, it was already present in all the Early Apostolic Church. It was the usual term for functions within the framework of the Church and not, significantly enough, for the services of one's neighbor or within the social orders. Διακονία is the service performed for the unifying and preservation of the Church, the service which establishes and maintains the faith; thus it is the office of the Church.[21]

God is speaking to today's church. The inscripturated revelation is His speaking voice.

This "good shepherd in the skies" yearns to shepherd people to Himself. He desires to guide, feed, and save people who are His sheep.

In the Old Testament, the Father is pictured as the Shepherd of Israel. In the New Testament, Jesus described Himself as the

---

20. Donald F. Thomas, *The Deacon in a Changing Church* (Valley Forge: Judson Press, 1969), p. 19.

21. Leonard Goppelt, *Apostolic and Post-Apostolic Times,* Trans. Robert A. Guelich (London: Adam & Charles Black, 1970), p. 177.

Good Shepherd. He trained His apostles to be shepherds of people. The apostles taught church leaders, overseers, elders and deacons in the shepherding ministry.

It is through the same leaders, today, that Christ continues His shepherding ministry.

Appendices

Appendix 1

An Affirmation of Our Faith

Adopted by the Baptist General Conference in 1951

1. The Word of God

We believe that the Bible is the Word of God, fully inspired and without error in the original manuscripts, written under the inspiration of the Holy Spirit, and that it has supreme authority in all matters of faith and conduct.

2. The Trinity

We believe that there is one living and true God, eternally existing in three persons; that these are equal in every divine perfection, and that they execute distinct but harmonious offices in the work of creation, providence and redemption.

3. God The Father

We believe in God, the Father, an infinite, personal spirit, perfect in holiness, wisdom, power and love. We believe that He concerns Himself mercifully in the affairs of men, that He hears and answers prayer, and that He saves from sin and death all who come to Him through Jesus Christ.

4. Jesus Christ

We believe in Jesus Christ, God's only begotten Son, conceived by the Holy Spirit. We believe in His virgin birth, sinless life, miracles and teachings. We believe in His substitutionary atoning death, bodily resurrection, ascension into heaven, perpetual intercession for His people, and personal visible return to earth.

5. The Holy Spirit

We believe in the Holy Spirit who came forth from the Father and Son to convict the world of sin, righteousness, and judgment, and to regenerate, sanctify, and empower all who believe in Jesus Christ. We believe that the Holy Spirit indwells every believer in Christ, and that He is an abiding helper, teacher and guide.

6. Regeneration

We believe that all men are sinners by nature and by choice and are, therefore, under condemnation. We believe that those who repent of their sins and trust in Jesus Christ as Savior are regenerated by the Holy Spirit.

7. The Church

We believe in the universal church, a living spiritual body of which Christ is the head and all regenerated persons are members. We believe in the local church, consisting of a company of believers in Jesus Christ, baptized on a credible profession of faith, and associated for worship, work and fellowship. We believe that God has laid upon the members of the local church the primary task of giving the Gospel of Jesus Christ to a lost world.

8. Christian Conduct

We believe that a Christian should live for the glory of God and the well being of his fellowmen; that his conduct should be blameless before the world; that he should be a faithful steward of his possessions; and that he should seek to realize for himself and others the full stature of maturity in Christ.

9. The Ordinances

We believe that the Lord Jesus Christ has committed two ordinances to the local church, baptism and the Lord's Supper. We believe that Christian baptism is the immersion of a believer in water into the name of the triune God. We believe that the Lord's Supper was instituted by Christ for commemoration of His death. We believe that these two ordinances should be observed and administered until the return of the Lord Jesus Christ.

10. Religious Liberty

We believe that every human being has direct relations with God, and is responsible to God alone in all matters of faith; that each church is independent and must be free from interference by any ecclesiastical or political authority; that therefore Church and State must be kept separate as having different functions, each fulfilling its duties free from dictation or patronage of the other.

11. Church Cooperation

We believe that local churches can best promote the cause of Jesus Christ by cooperating with one another in a denominational organization. Such an organization, whether a regional or district conference, exists and functions by the will of the churches. Cooperation in a conference is voluntary and may be terminated at any time. Churches may likewise cooperate with inter-denominational fellowships on a voluntary independent basis.

12. The Last Things

We believe in the personal and visible return of the Lord Jesus Christ to earth and the establishment of His kingdom. We believe in the resurrection of the body, the final judgment, the eternal felicity of the righteous, and the endless suffering of the wicked.

Appendix 2

Bible Reading

Paragraph Title Record

THURSDAY   Date _____ Today's Paragraph_____
1. Main idea of the paragraph in title form (eight words or less)
TITLE:_____

_____

2. The idea's application to my life: _____

_____

_____

FRIDAY   Date _____ Today's Paragraph_____
1. Main idea of the paragraph in title form (eight words or less)
TITLE:_____

_____

2. The idea's application to my life: _____

_____

_____

SATURDAY   Date _____ Today's Paragraph_____
1. Main idea of the paragraph in title form (eight words or less)
TITLE:_____

_____

2. The idea's application to my life: _____

_____

_____

Appendix 3

Little Flock Section

Basic Requirements for *Overseeing* Your Little Flock

1. A minimum of a corporate little flock gathering at least once each three months.

    a. This will be primarily social with its objective the building of relationship to develop a support group for the members of the little flock.

    b. It can be a covered dish dinner. The Lind Room can be used. Back yard home gatherings are better as the weather permits. Picnic, ball games and other group interest opportunities can be used.

2. The establishment of a meaningful pastoral relationship between the lay shepherd and each member of his flock. The members of the flock, in time, will turn to the lay shepherds first in crisis. Then the lay shepherds will contact the church office and pastoral staff.

3. A hospital call must be made by the lay shepherd on each member of his little flock who is hospitalized.

    Books to take as gifts will be available. They are in the closet behind the bi-fold doors in the Conference room.

4. One man and his wife are to be selected by the shepherding team to be discipled as understudies in shepherding. This will require at least a monthly meeting with the understudies to share in brief the general content of the weekly training sessions and share and pray for the needs of the little flock as well as plan a future ministry to them.

5. A home communion service with the little flock led by the lay shepherd will be held at least once each year.

Appendix 4

Report Form of Little Flock Ministries by The Shepherding Teams

1. This form may be filled out by the Deacon or Deaconess. Please collaborate on the material put down.

2. Next Wednesday evening, April 25, will be report night. All Deacons and Deaconesses are urged to be in attendance. Either the Deacon or Deaconess will share in summary the material of the year's activities from the report form. Dessert will be served—it should be a good evening. If you cannot be there, see that the report is in the office by May 1.

3. List the approximate dates of times you've had Little Flock get-togethers, what they were (potlucks, etc.) and the approximate number in attendance.

_____   _____   _____

_____   _____   _____

_____   _____   _____

_____   _____   _____

_____   _____   _____

_____   _____   _____

4. List individual ministries that you can recall like home calls, hospital calls, luncheon appointments, telephone calls, etc.

_____

_____

_____

_____

_____

_____

_____

_____

_____

5. Write a paragraph about one shepherding incident in your Little Flock ministry that was especially rewarding and heart-warming to you.

Appendix 5

Shepherding Report

Visit Little Flock Home

Date _____

Shepherding Team_____

Home Visited _____

Evaluate Call _____

_____

_____

_____

_____

_____

_____

_____

_____

_____

Scripture Used _____

Check if closed with prayer _____

Reflection—what spiritual needs surfaced or were made more apparent to you because of the call: _____

_____

_____

Signed:

_____

Appendix 6

The Role of the Undershepherding Team

Exodus 18:24; II Timothy 2:2

The Shepherding Team will select another husband-wife combination to work as helpers in various ministries to the flock.

1. This ministry may lead to a full shepherding role with election as a deacon and deaconess, but it isn't necessarily a first step in that direction. The assisting team may be chosen because of their gifts which would augment those of the Shepherding Team. For example, the Shepherdess does not feel strong gifts in entertaining or organizing for dinners and social affairs. A man doesn't feel strong alone. They see a couple that have both these gifts and would be willing to serve in those areas and assist. They are asked to do so.

2. It would be a tremendous help to the Shepherding Team if they would share the responsibility of the flock with the Undershepherding Team. With the Shepherding Teams taking six households and the Undershepherding Teams six households for fellowship or prayer gatherings, the division of labor and a more flexible grouping would be the result.

3. Perhaps the Shepherding Team and the Undershepherding Team could share the list, six and six for telephoning. Checking up in case of absence, etc.

4. A once a month meeting with the two teams would enable the Shepherd and Shepherdess to share the Wednesday night training session and what is taking place there. It would also enable them to begin discipling the undershepherding team if they are responsive.

Bibliography

Books

Adams, Jay E. *Pastoral Leadership*. Grand Rapids: Baker Book House, 1975.

> The third in a series under the overarching theme, "Shepherding God's Flock." The book is addressed to pastors, but the principles of the book and much of its material is applicable to lay leaders.

Adams, Jay E. *The Pastoral Life*. Grand Rapids: Baker Book House, 1975.

> This is the first in a series on shepherding God's flock. It introduces the subject of pastoral theology and then gives a very good overview of shepherd life and care. It is addressed to pastors.

Baumann, Dan, *All Originality Makes A Dull Church*. Santa Ana: Vision House Publishers, 1976.

> The author depicts five styles of churches, giving a case study on nine. He believes that all lessons learned by a local fellowship ought to be common property of the body of Christ.

Clebsch, William A., and Jackle, Charles R. *Pastoral Care In Historical Perspective*. Englewood Cliffs: Prentice Hall, 1964.

> The book has excellent definitions of pastoral care from a technical perspective.

Dudley, Carl S. *Making the Small Church Effective*. Nashville: Abingdon, 1978.

> The author makes a compelling case for the place of a small church in our society.

Feucht, Oscar E. *Everyone A Minister*. Philadelphia: Westminster Press, 1974.

> This book is a guide to churchmanship for laity and clergy. It sets forth in practical terms the startling possibility of a biblically-inspired priesthood of believers.

99

Getz, Gene A. *Sharpening The Focus of The Church.* Chicago: Moody Press, 1974.

The author discusses why the church exists, how to build the church through New Testament principles, administration, and organization.

Goppelt, Leonard. *Apostolic and Post-Apostolic Times.* Translated by Robert A. Guelich. London: Adam & Charles Black, 1970.

Fine scholarship recounts the development of the church and her message in the first century.

Griffiths, Michael. *God's Forgetful Pilgrims.* Grand Rapids: Wm. B. Eerdman's Publishing Co., 1979.

This excellent biblical study emphasizes the church as a body and its need for growth and development corporately.

Jefferson, Charles. *The Minister As Shepherd.* Manila: Living Books for All, 1973.

This is the most heart-warming book that I've read on shepherding and pastoral care. It reminds the reader of his responsibilities as one of God's shepherds to do a better job. It is a convicting book.

Keller, Phillip. *A Shepherd Looks at Psalm 23.* Grand Rapids: Zondervan Publishing House, 1970.

An excellent devotional book with remarkable insights on shepherding by an author who was a shepherd of sheep.

Kittel, G., and Friedrich, G., editors. *Theological Dictionary Of The New Testament.* 9 Vols. Grand Rapids: Eerdmans, 1968.

A superb source for word study in the original language. The writers trace the development of a word under study from its classical period through its development in scriptural usage.

Kraemer, Hendrick. *A Theology of Laity.* Philadelphia: Westminster Press, 1958.

A very insightful overview of the history and theology of a lay person's role.

Miguens, Manuel. *Church Ministries In New Testament Times.* Westminster, Md.: Christian Classics, 1976.

A fine study of official order with the duties of offices in the Christian community in the New Testament and patristic periods.

Perry, Lloyd. *Getting the Church on Target.* Chicago: Moody Press, 1977.

The author outlines ways in which the local church can be revitalized. Chapter four deals with developing a church's organizational structure. It is a well-balanced book with excellent help in the "How To's" of leadership.

67739

Schweizer, Edward. *Church Order in the New Testament*. Naperville, Ill.: Alec R. Allenson, 1961.

> This book provides excellent materials for the various stages of development in the first-century church. It presents a strong case for the great diversity and variety of New Testament churches.

Scipion, George. *Timothy, Titus, and You*. Phillipsburg, N.J.: Pilgrim Publishing Co., 1975.

> This is an excellent manual designed to train elders (or potential elders). It takes elders through all the potential passages pertaining to their qualifications and ministry. Each lesson has a homework assignment.

Sider, Ronald J. *Rich Christians in an Age of Hunger*. Downers Grove: Inter-Varsity Press, 1977.

Stedman, Ray C. *Body Life*. Glendale: Regal Books, 1972.

> The author makes an excellent case for a participatory fellowship that embodies New Testament *koinonia*. It is a "How To" book on church relationships.

Stowe, Eugene L. *The Ministry of Shepherding*. Kansas City: Beacon Hill Press, 1976.

> This book is a study on pastoral care from the senior pastor's perspective.

Thomas, Donald F. *The Deacon in a Changing Church*. Valley Forge: Judson Press, 1969.

> The book is written to give assistance to lay leadership in a world of change. The beginning dealing with biblical principles for the ministry of the diaconate is insightful.

von Campenhausen, Hans. *Ecclesiastical Authority and Spiritual Power*. Stanford: Stanford University Press, 1969.

> The author does a scholarly work of developing the offices of the church and their authority into the patristic period. The book is of extreme importance in understanding the power structure of the early church.

Unpublished Material

Bailey, David D. "Manual for Lay Ministers of Pastoral Care." Paper used in the training program of the Garden Grove Community Church of Garden Grove, Calif. (Mimeographed.)

> Contains the overview of the entire lay ministry program of the Garden Grove Community Church, its training materials and sample correspondence.

Bixley, Howard. "Deacon Caring Kit." Material used by Calvary Baptist Church. Grand Rapids, 1979. (Tapes.)

> Six cassette tapes explain the Deacon Caring Ministry of Calvary Baptist Church of Grand Rapids, Michigan. The material is helpful in the practical "How To" of developing a deacon ministry.

Board of Education of the UPCUSA. "The Ministry of the Deacons in the UPCUSA Today." Philadelphia, 1963.

> A collection of seven unpublished manuscripts presented at a consultation held July 15-19, 1964, prior to the report on "The Nature of the Ministry" made to the 176th General Assembly of the United Presbyterian Churches in the United States of America. The recommendation was made that the lay office of deacon be abolished in favor of using that title to designate a form of clerical ministry. The manuscripts provide a wealth of material on many different aspects of the diaconate. Titles include: "Lay Ordination in the New Testament Context"; "The Problem of the Diaconate"; "Lay Ordination and the Diaconate"; "The Diaconate in the Reformed Tradition"; "An Interpretation of the Diaconate in the Light of Pre-Reformation Church History"; and "The Role of the Diaconate in the Contemporary Church."

Ver Straten, Charles. "Changing Baptist Deacons into Lay Shepherds." Denver: Conservative Baptist Theological Seminary, 1980. (Doctoral dissertation.)

> This is the documentation of the project which gave birth to this book.

——. *Shepherding Notebook*. Littleton, Colo.: Mission Hills Baptist Church, 1979.